The Cat Basket

Books by Vernon Coleman

The Medicine Men (1975)
Paper Doctors (1976)
Everything You Want To Know About Ageing (1976)
Stress Control (1978)
The Home Pharmacy (1980)
Aspirin or Ambulance (1980)
Face Values (1981)
Guilt (1982)
The Good Medicine Guide (1982)
Stress And Your Stomach (1983)
Bodypower (1983)
An A to Z Of Women's Problems (1984)
Bodysense (1984)
Taking Care Of Your Skin (1984)
A Guide to Child Health (1984)
Life Without Tranquillisers (1985)
Diabetes (1985)
Arthritis (1985)
Eczema and Dermatitis (1985)
The Story Of Medicine (1985, 1998)
Natural Pain Control (1986)
Mindpower (1986)
Addicts and Addictions (1986)
Dr Vernon Coleman's Guide To Alternative Medicine (1988)
Stress Management Techniques (1988)
Overcoming Stress (1988)
Know Yourself (1988)
The Health Scandal (1988)
The 20 Minute Health Check (1989)
Sex For Everyone (1989)
Mind Over Body (1989)
Eat Green Lose Weight (1990)
Why Animal Experiments Must Stop (1991)
The Drugs Myth (1992)
How To Overcome Toxic Stress (1990)
Why Doctors Do More Harm Than Good (1993)
Stress and Relaxation (1993)

Complete Guide To Sex (1993)
How to Conquer Backache (1993)
How to Conquer Arthritis (1993)
Betrayal of Trust (1994)
Know Your Drugs (1994, 1997)
Food for Thought (1994, revised edition 2000)
The Traditional Home Doctor (1994)
I Hope Your Penis Shrivels Up (1994)
People Watching (1995)
Relief from IBS (1995)
The Parent's Handbook (1995)
Oral Sex: Bad Taste And Hard To Swallow? (1995)
Why Is Pubic Hair Curly? (1995)
Men in Dresses (1996)
Power over Cancer (1996)
Crossdressing (1996)
How to Conquer Arthritis (1996)
High Blood Pressure (1996)
How To Stop Your Doctor Killing You (1996, revised edition 2003)
Fighting For Animals (1996)
Alice and Other Friends (1996)
Spiritpower (1997)
Other People's Problems (1998)
How To Publish Your Own Book (1999)
How To Relax and Overcome Stress (1999)
Animal Rights – Human Wrongs (1999)
Superbody (1999)
The 101 Sexiest, Craziest, Most Outrageous Agony Column
        Questions (and Answers) of All Time (1999)
Strange But True (2000)
Daily Inspirations (2000)
Stomach Problems: Relief At Last (2001)
How To Overcome Guilt (2001)
How To Live Longer (2001)
Sex (2001)
How To Make Money While Watching TV (2001)
We Love Cats (2002)
England Our England (2002)
Rogue Nation (2003)

People Push Bottles Up Peaceniks (2003)
The Cats' Own Annual (2003)
Confronting The Global Bully (2004)
Saving England (2004)
Why Everything Is Going To Get Worse Before It Gets Better (2004)
The Secret Lives of Cats (2004)
The Cat Basket (2005)

novels
The Village Cricket Tour (1990)
The Bilbury Chronicles (1992)
Bilbury Grange (1993)
Mrs Caldicot's Cabbage War (1993)
Bilbury Revels (1994)
Deadline (1994)
The Man Who Inherited a Golf Course (1995)
Bilbury Country (1996)
Second Innings (1999)
Around the Wicket (2000)
It's Never Too Late (2001)
Paris In My Springtime (2002)
Mrs Caldicot's Knickerbocker Glory (2003)
Too Many Clubs And Not Enough Balls (2005)

short stories
Bilbury Pie (1995)

on cricket
Thomas Winsden's Cricketing Almanack (1983)
Diary Of A Cricket Lover (1984)

as Edward Vernon
Practice Makes Perfect (1977)
Practise What You Preach (1978)
Getting Into Practice (1979)
Aphrodisiacs – An Owner's Manual (1983)
The Complete Guide To Life (1984)

with Alice
Alice's Diary (1989)
Alice's Adventures (1992)

with Dr Alan C Turin
No More Headaches (1981)

With Donna Antoinette Coleman
How To Conquer Health Problems Between Ages 50 and 120 (2003)
Health Secrets Doctors Share With Their Families (2005)

The Cat Basket

Vernon Coleman

Decorated by the author

Chilton Designs

Published by Chilton Designs, Publishing House, Trinity Place, Barnstaple, Devon EX32 9HG, England

ISBN: 1 898146 85 3

A catalogue record for this book is available from the British Library.

Printed and bound in the UK by Arrowsmith, Bristol

Contents

Author's Note

The Cat Basket is dedicated to Donna Antoinette, my adorable Welsh Princess, who is enough of a cataholic to choose to come back as a cat, enough of a romantic to prefer to be a white, fluffy one and wise enough to insist on coming back in the care of an Upright who adores all cats but has a special soft spot for white fluffy ones. I hope she enjoys curling up with *The Cat Basket* for a while. And I hope you do too. Welcome, once again, to my cat world.

Vernon Coleman March 2005

P.S. As readers of my other cat books will know I use the word 'Upright' instead of the phrase 'human being'. The word was first used in this way by Alice in her two books *Alice's Diary* and *Alice's Adventures* and I have adopted it and used it, in her memory, ever since.

"My name is Vernon, and I'm a cataholic"

Chapter One

The Telepathic Link Between Cats And Uprights

Many Uprights who have lived with one or more cats will confirm that a telepathic link often exists between cats and Uprights.

(A telepathic link, I should perhaps explain, is defined as 'communication by a method which does not rely upon the senses'. It is, in other words, a form of communication which does not rely on sight, hearing, smell, taste or touch.)

Only through the existence of a telepathic link between Uprights and cats can otherwise inexplicable events be satisfactorily explained.

However much sceptics may sneer (and they definitely do and certainly will) there is just too much anecdotal evidence supporting the existence of a telepathic link for the hypothesis to be dismissed. There is no doubt that a telepathic bond does exist between cats and Uprights and that the telepathic bond can stretch over great distances – often over hundreds of miles.

There are, I believe, numerous ways in which the telepathic link between Uprights and cats manifests itself. I have, below, defined five specific variations on this theme.

1. Uprights Can Call Cats By Using Telepathy

There is an astonishing amount of evidence to support the claim that Uprights can contact cats by telepathy. For example, many Uprights have reported that when they want to attract their cat's attention they only have to think hard – rather than go outside and call the cat's name. 'It's a bit like tuning in to the radio,' explained one Upright. 'I just think hard about my cat and within a minute or two she will suddenly come running.' A woman who lives in Michigan, USA, and who has five cats reports that if her cats are out of the house she only has to think of one of the cats and that cat will appear at her door. A woman in Jerusalem says that she used to have to call her cat when she got home from work but that these days all she has to do is *think* about calling the cat. The cat then appears. This is something that any reader with a cat can try quite easily. It might not work straight away (the channels through which telepathy operates might need reviving) but it's an experiment which costs nothing and has no known hazards.

2. Cats Can Use Telepathy To Contact Uprights

Just as there is evidence to show that Uprights can call cats using telepathy so there is evidence showing that cats can call Uprights. Sometimes telepathy is used for fairly trivial reasons. For example, one man reports that he woke early one morning and suddenly said to his wife: 'The cat wants to come in.' He got up and looked out of the window. There, sitting on the drive was their cat. The cat was looking up at the bedroom window. The man went downstairs, opened the door and let the cat in. This has now become quite routine. The cat, it seems, has managed to tune into the man's brain and can send him messages whenever he wants to.

Sometimes, telepathy is used for more urgent purposes. One woman's cat escaped from a local cattery. No one knew where it had gone. Desperate and distraught the woman got into her car and drove around lanes she didn't know. Suddenly she stopped and opened the car door. Her cat, previously unseen, calmly got into the vehicle and lay down. Another woman reports that when she lost her cat she simply sat and tried to 'think' about where her cat might be. She thought she saw her cat locked in a nearby garage. She went to the owner of the garage and asked him to open it. The cat, which had been accidentally locked in, was sitting inside waiting for her. A third woman who lost her cat searched unsuccessfully and was about to give up. She sat down, thinking of her cat. Moments later she got up, walked to a house half a street away and asked the owners if she could look in their garden. When she walked down the garden path and called her cat she heard a miaow. She found her cat, unable to move, stuck in a pile of rubbish.

3. Cats Know When Their Uprights Are Coming Home

There is a mass of evidence to support this claim and hundreds of Uprights have confirmed that when they arrive home their cat will always be waiting for them in exactly the same place – at a window, behind the door or near a gate. Some cats will meet their favourite Upright on the way home, or wait at a bus stop or railway station. In most cases the cat concerned will wait only for one person – the person to whom they are most closely attached. Other Uprights in the household have confirmed that the cat will go and sit by the door or window just minutes before the arrival of a specific Upright and that this happens before any sounds can be heard and even when the Upright's homecoming is unpredictable and erratic. Generally speaking, cats tend to start waiting less than ten minutes before the arrival of the Upright. The cat's decision to wait cannot be explained by routine or the sound of an approaching engine.

A young man whose father had a job which meant that he had unpredictable hours reports that: 'My mother knew to put my father's meal in the oven when the cat suddenly looked up, got up and trotted to the front gate. She knew that the cat's movement meant that my father was on his way home.'

A woman whose cats always knew when she was coming home and would go to the door to wait for her was told by her husband one evening: 'The cats got it wrong tonight. They were restless at nine o'clock so I expected you home half an hour ago.' It was 9.40 pm at the time. The woman thought for a moment and then told her husband that she had left her meeting at 9 o'clock and had got into her car ready to drive home. 'But I suddenly remembered something I had to do,' she said. 'So I had to pop back for a moment. I ended up staying an extra thirty minutes.' The cats hadn't got it wrong at all. They had, quite accurately, responded to her leaving the meeting and had continued to wait for her.

A man in Argentina had a cat which slept on his bed at night. If the man's teenage son was out of the house the cat would jump off the bed and go and wait by the front door a few minutes before the boy arrived home by taxi. The cat would ignore taxis which did not contain the boy and go downstairs only for the arrival of the correct taxi.

A woman left Switzerland to live in Paris and had to leave her cat behind with her mother. After the daughter had left the cat disappeared. No one knew where it was living. But every two or three months when the young woman returned home to Switzerland the cat knew that she was coming and reappeared. It was well-fed and cared for. The cat would disappear again when the young woman went back to Paris. One day the cat suddenly appeared on the mother's doorstep. The mother thought that the cat had made a mistake because she was not expecting her daughter to visit. A little later the daughter appeared, making an (to everyone except the cat) unexpected visit.

A doctor in Switzerland reports that when his family go away on holiday they arrange to leave their cat with their neighbours. On the day when they are due to come back from their holiday the cat always leaves the neighbour's house and goes to wait for its own Uprights at their home.

A couple who live on the English south coast went on holiday for two weeks leaving their cat with an aunt who lived a couple of miles away from them. When the couple got back home they found their cat sitting on their gatepost waiting for them. They rang their aunt to thank her for looking after the cat. The aunt was frantic. The cat had disappeared that morning. Somehow it had known that its Uprights were coming back and had gone to their house to wait for them.

4. Cats Know When Their Uprights Are Injured (Or Worse)

Cats who are closely attached to Uprights will often show signs of distress if something happens to their Upright. They will respond to distant deaths and emergencies with howling, whining and plaintive miaowing. Often, other Uprights around the cat may be puzzled by its apparently inexplicable behaviour.

A German woman reports that she was sitting on her verandah with her three-year-old Persian cat when suddenly the cat jumped up, uttered a strange cry and rushed into the living room where she sat by the telephone. Moments later the telephone rang with news that the woman's daughter had had a bicycle accident and had been taken to hospital.

A couple in Switzerland had a son and a cat. The cat was very attached to the boy who went away to work on a ship. Whenever the boy came home (his visits were always irregular and unexpected) the cat would be waiting at the door of his room. One day the cat went to the door of the son's room and sat there miaowing miserably, clearly distressed. Two days later the couple were told that their son had died at sea. He had died, they discovered, at the very moment when the cat had gone to the door of his room. He had been 7,000 miles away at the time.

A woman and her husband went to Denmark on holiday. While in Denmark the husband, who was quite young, had a heart attack and died. The couple's cat, who was being looked after by a friend, went into a corner and whined at the very moment when the husband died. The woman who was looking after the cat said that she knew that something terrible had happened because the cat's whole body was shaking.

Sometimes, a cat's perceptive powers may mean that it is aware of things that the Upright concerned does not know about. For example, an English woman who suffers from epilepsy has a cat which warns her when she is about to have a fit. 'About an hour before a fit starts,' says the woman, 'the cat will come to me and touch my face gently with her paw. She will keep doing this every few seconds or so and won't let me out of her sight. She will stay with me throughout my fit and will be there, waiting, when I wake up.'

Other Uprights have described how cats have fetched help or have stood guard over someone who has collapsed.

And the type of telepathic relationship I have just described works the other way round, too. Uprights have reported that they have suddenly been overwhelmed with a sense of great sadness and have later discovered that at that moment something terrible has happened to a favourite cat.

5. Cats Will Respond When A Favourite Upright Calls By Phone

It is remarkable enough that cats will know when an Upright is approaching. Even more remarkably cats will often be aware when a favoured Upright is on the telephone. They will ignore phone calls from strangers and then rush towards the telephone instrument when it rings with a call from a loved Upright. As if that wasn't extraordinary enough it has been reported that some cats will go and sit by a phone just before it starts to ring – with a favoured Upright making the call, of course.

* * *

Telepathy is a communications tool about which we know very little. (I have explored this phenomenon in one or two of my medical books.)

But nowhere is the power of telepathy better illustrated than between loved cats and their loving Uprights. The bond between cat and Upright can indeed be a close one.

You might find it rewarding to explore your own relationship with a cat. How close are you? What links are there that you have not yet explored? How can you use, develop and expand those links?

Chairman Miaow

Chapter Two

How To Tell If You're A Cataholic

Answer the questions below as honestly and as accurately as you can. All you have to do is choose just one of the four possible answers to each question. Make a note of your choices and then, at the end of the questionnaire, check your score. As always, with questionnaires of this type, there are no 'right' or 'wrong' answers. Your responses will be treated confidentially unless you tick or circle the answer you've chosen, and then leave the book lying around in which case it really isn't my fault.

1. At Christmas would you prefer to receive a card illustrated with:
a)   an obese Father Christmas scoffing mince pies and swigging sherry
b)   a rude cartoon which plays a seasonal tune when you open it
c)   a drawing of a Dickensian street covered in snow
d)   a photograph of a fluffy kitten looking utterly adorable

2. How many pictures or models of cats do you have in your home:
a)   none
b)   one or two
c)   quite a few
d)   too many to count

3. How often do you talk about cats:
a) never
b) rarely
c) frequently
d) as often as possible

4. If you are on a stroll in the country and you see a cat sitting on a wall would you:
a) hurry on by
b) nod in passing
c) smile and say 'hello'
d) stop and stroke the cat

5. If you are rushing somewhere to an important appointment and you see a cat sitting on a wall would you:
a) hurry on by
b) nod in passing
c) smile and say 'hello'
d) stop and stroke the cat

6. If choosing a birthday card would you choose one illustrated with:
a) a bottle of champagne with the cork popping out
b) a bunch of flowers in a vase
c) a picture of a small harbour with colourful boats
d) a picture of a cat not doing anything

7. How often do you think about cats:
a) once a year
b) once a month
c) once a week
d) more than the above

8. How often do you dream about cats:
a) once in a blue moon
b) every now and then
c) when there's an 'r' in the month
d) not as often as I'd like

9. If you had to be stranded on a desert island what would you choose to take with you:

a) eight gramophone records
b) an ironing board
c) a bucket and spade
d) a cat of your choice

10. What would you prefer to watch on television:

a) a documentary about Polish steel workers in the 1930s
b) a party political broadcast
c) a reality television show in which foul mouthed nonentities get drunk and complain about the food they've been given to eat
d) cats and kittens playing in a country garden

11. You can share your life with one animal. Which animal would you choose from the following list:

a) a large dog with sharp teeth and a tendency to growl at anything that moves
b) a koala bear (careful now)
c) a pet rat
d) a fluffy cat with twinkly eyes and a loveable personality

12. Which of these do you think would make the best pet for a small child:

a) a boa constrictor
b) a goldfish
c) a pit bull terrier
d) a nice cat

Now check your score and find out whether or not you're a cataholic. Give yourself 5 points for every time you chose answer d) to a question. Give yourself 0 points for every other answer you chose.

If you scored 0-15:

There is no need for you to feel particularly ashamed by your score but you don't fit in very well and you are a bit of a worry to us. Maybe you weren't feeling well when you completed the questionnaire. More likely, perhaps you simply didn't understand the questions. Perhaps it would be a good idea for you to try again. Repeat the whole exercise and see if you can get a better score second time round. (Tip: if you look to see which questions carry top marks you will see where you've been going wrong.)

If you scored 20 to 35:

You're probably quite a nice person in some ways and, given time, you will undoubtedly mature into the sort of person we'd all like you to be. Meanwhile, you need to look carefully at your life to see where you're going wrong. A little critical self-assessment never hurt anyone. Go through the questionnaire again and find out where you lost points. It shouldn't be too difficult for you to decide how to improve your score.

If you scored 40 to 60

You're a lovely person; kind, thoughtful, affectionate and caring. You are sensitive, intelligent, perspicacious, graceful and loyal. You are, in a word, a cataholic. (And special congratulations to you if you obtained the maximum score of 60.)

"Can I be your friend?"

Chapter Three

Three Dozen Assorted And Amazing Catfacts Every Cat Lover Should Know

1. Cats have lived with humans for at least 5,000 years and were first domesticated in North Africa. (Readers who like impressing their friends might like to note that the wild ancestor of the first domesticated cat was the African wild cat Felis Silvestris.)

2. The Ancient Egyptians (who weren't ancient at the time, of course) revered cats and happily shared their homes with them. They regarded domestic cats as the living embodiments of the cat goddess known as Bastest.

3. The original English cats were coloured blue-black and white.

4. Cats are very popular in France. The French may not have much of a reputation as animal lovers (vegetarianism is almost unknown and large numbers of Frenchmen spend their weekends wandering across the countryside shooting anything – including other Frenchmen – that moves) but they do adore cats. Indeed, they love them so much that the statistics show that one person in two in France sleeps with a cat. (So much for the reputation of the French as great lovers. It is difficult to be romantic when there is a cat sleeping on or in the bed.)

5. Tabby cats were first introduced into Britain in the 1630s.

6. In AD 948 a Welsh King known as Howell the Good used to sell young kittens for a penny each. Once a kitten had caught its first mouse its value increased and the price went up to two pence.

7. All kittens have blue eyes.

8. It is a myth that cats can see in total darkness. They can't. However, cats do have very good night vision and in dim light their vision is about half as good again as that of the average clear-sighted human being.

9. Cats pee in shoes because they want to hide the evidence so that predators won't be able to find them easily. Shoes tend to offer the smelliest spot in the house – the place where their own tell-tale smell is least likely to be noticed.

10. Siamese cats sometimes have a genetic fault which produces double vision. When a cat tries to correct this the result is the characteristic Siamese squint.

11. A cat's ears are able to rotate through 180 degrees. This gives hunting cats an enormous advantage and enables them to hear and locate their prey more easily.

12. The soft pad of a cat's nose is sensitive to cold. This is why a cat will often bury its nose in its tail fur.

13. Human mothers who breast-feed pass on protective antibodies to their babies. Cats are the same. When a kitten feeds on its mother's milk it acquires antibodies which help to give it protection from disease.

14. Cats prefer to attack from behind for two reasons. First, an attack from the fear gives them an element of surprise. Second, their claws work more efficiently if the prey is attempting to flee.

15. Cats obtain enormous pleasure from grooming themselves. They don't just do it to get clean – they do it because they like doing it. It is, perhaps, a reminder of the comforts of kittenhood. It makes

them feel safe and relaxed in the same way that a kitten feels safe and relaxed when it is being groomed by its mother. There is a third reason why cats lick themselves so much; sebum secreted in their hair follicles is a valuable source of vitamin D.

16. Kittens really need the care and attention they get from their mothers. Kittens who have not been taught how to hunt by their mothers grow up to be either uninterested in hunting or very bad at it. Kittens who don't know how to hunt tend to become rather bored in adulthood. It is almost as if they have been robbed of their main purpose in life. And kittens which miss out on other aspects of their training from their mother grow up to be dysfunctional; they may have difficulty fitting in with other cats because they haven't been taught how to behave. For this reason kittens should be at least 10 weeks old (and preferably 12 weeks old) before they are parted from their mothers and found new homes.

17. The ideal two-cat household consists of two kittens from the same litter. They will grow up used to one another and comfortable with one another's little ways.

18. Neutering tends to make cats more home-loving and less inclined to wander.

19. When domestic cats knead with their front paws, they are exhibiting an instinctive infantile reaction known as 'milk treadling' – designed to stimulate lactation.

20. Play fighting between young cats or between a kitten and its parents is a vital part of growing up. It is through play fighting that kittens and young cats learn the coordination and timing needed for hunting effectively. Play fighting also teaches a cat the moves it may need to defend itself if it is attacked later in life.

21. Cats only bury their faeces when they feel it might otherwise betray the whereabouts of their den (or, with domestic cats, their home). Otherwise the remains are left uncovered as a territorial scent mark.

22. Most cat species prefer a solitary existence. The practical explanation for this is that the available prey in a given area can only support a limited number of individuals. The more cats there are in an area the more cats there will be to share out a finite number of mice.

23. A queen will miss her kittens when they are taken from her and should be given extra treats and comforts for a few days. Strangely, a queen will not acknowledge her kittens as her own offspring if she meets them again after a period of separation. (This is in stark contrast to other animals. For example, if a ewe meets a lamb from whom she has been parted for several years she will greet her 'baby' with great joy and affection.)

24. Tortoiseshell domestic cats are nearly always female. This is because the genes which result in these colours are activated by an X chromosome combination.

25. Feral male cats invariably live solitary lives but feral females often live in a small group, particularly when living on a farm or in some other specific group of buildings. Feral females often live with feral females (mothers and daughters) from other litters in a sort of female commune. In social circumstances like this one feral female will happily care for the kittens of another – even suckling another queen's kittens.

26. In 1950 a Swiss kitten managed to follow a group of climbers right to the summit of the Matterhorn in the Alps. The summit of the Matterhorn is 14,691 ft (4,478m) high.

27. Cats are not pack animals and so, unlike dogs, they have no need to impress anyone. This is why cats are disinclined to obey instructions. A dog will learn tricks because it wants to impress its (human) pack leader. A cat doesn't give a stuff about impressing anyone.

28. The tail is a very important feature for some species of cat. Those species which need to climb trees or pursue prey at speed will use their tail to help them balance.

29. The stripy and blotchy markings on cats' coats are there as camouflage. They help to break up the cat's outline and work in just the same way as camouflage clothing worn by soldiers.

30. The affectionate words 'mog' and 'moggie' (or 'moggy'), which are often used to describe domestic cats originated in England as affectionate slang names for the cow. The yokel who first mistook his cat for a cow must have been well lubricated on local cider.

31. The only breed of cat which enjoys water (and is a good swimmer) is the Turkish Van. The Turkish Van has an all-white coat relieved only by patches of colour on its head, and a coloured tail which may be decorated with darker coloured rings.

32. Don't use old newspapers as cat bedding. The paper and the ink may contain harmful chemicals. A recent authoritative survey published in a leading mewspaper for cats showed that most cats prefer bedding made of blankets, cushions and old jumpers which smell of their favourite Upright. Bedding should not be washed with powerful soap powders (which might cause allergy problems) but in safe hypoallergenic products.

33. The abdomen of a cat is the animal's most vulnerable area. When a cat rolls over and exposes his or her abdomen, it is displaying a great deal of trust. Alice was one of the few cats I've known who used to love having her tummy tickled. She would roll onto her back, with her paws in the air, and wait to have her tummy rubbed.

34. The whiskers on the face of a cat form a unique pattern. The whisker pattern gives each cat a 'fingerprint' from which it could be positively identified.

35. Cats usually yawn in order to draw extra oxygen into their lungs. They want the extra oxygen to help them digest a heavy meal while they have a doze. Cats don't bother yawning if they are tired – they just go to sleep.

36. On the Royal Tombs at Thebes there is an inscription which reads:
    'Thou art the great cat, the avenger of the gods, and the judge of
    words, and the President of the sovereign chiefs and the Governor
    of the Holy Circle; thou art indeed...the Great Cat.'

Chapter Four

So, You Thought *You* Were Potty About Cats!

When you next find yourself spoiling a cat, or fear that you are becoming a little obsessed by cats in general, read this section and take comfort from the fact that you are most definitely not alone.

Here are short pieces about ten famous people whom you might not expect to have been completely potty about cats but who most definitely were, and who all deserve the respect and admiration of cat lovers everywhere.

1. Cardinal Richelieu

Powerful and hard as steel Armand Jean du Plessis (also and much better known as Cardinal Richelieu) was Louis XIII's chief minister. He was the most feared politician in 17th century France, crushing rivals and enemies such as the Habsburgs and Huguenots with impunity, but he was also gloriously potty about cats.

Richelieu may have ruled the roost everywhere else but at home his 14 cats were in charge. Wherever he went around the palace they would follow in a wonderful feline procession. Two palace attendants were hired exclusively to look after them.

Cardinal Richelieu gave his cats amazing names. The cat who usually slept on his lap was called Soumise. The best ratter was called Ludovic the Cruel and a jet black cat was known as Lucifer. He had cats called Gazette, Pyramus, Rita, Rubis, Serpolet and Thisbe. Richelieu founded the Academie Française and two of his cats, who were born in a wig (perruque) which the Marquis de Racan had left lying around and which their mother had adopted as a nest, were named Racan and Perruque.

In his will, Cardinal Richelieu left each one of his cats – and their attendants – sizeable pensions so that they could live on in luxurious splendour.

2. Edward Lear

Edward Lear, the English artist and humorist began his professional life travelling around Europe painting landscapes for his patron the Earl of Derby. When at home he entertained the Earl's children with limericks and silly verse which he illustrated himself with cartoon sketches. Lear had a striped tom cat called Foss, who was the inspiration for his famous rhyme *The Owl and the Pussy Cat*. Lear spent most of his later years in Italy and when he moved to San Remo in Italy in 1881 he had a new house built to exactly the same specification as the one he had left so that Foss would feel at home and know his way about. Foss's tombstone records that he was 31 years old when he died and that he had lived with Lear for 30 years.

3. Dr Samuel Johnson

Dr Samuel Johnson, English writer, critic, lexicographer, famed as the subject of James Boswell's biography and creator of the Dictionary of the English Language had many cats including one called Hodge which was fed on a diet of oysters. The great Dr Johnson went out every day and fetched Hodge's oysters himself because he worried that if he sent the servants out on this errand they might feel resentful and grow to dislike Hodge.

4. Admiral Horatio Nelson

In 1797 a flighty bit and professional mistress called Emma Hamilton found a stray kitten in the courtyard of the British Embassy in Naples. She called it Tiddles and adopted it as a pet. When she returned to England with her lover Admiral Viscount Horatio Nelson, Emma took the cat with them (there were no daft quarantine regulations then) and gave the cat to Nelson (who had become her husband) as a present in

1803. Nelson loved the cat so much that he took it with him when he went away to sea and Tiddles was on HMS Victory with Nelson at the Battle of Trafalgar in 1805. After Nelson died Tiddles moved to HMS Amphion. Tiddles died in action at the siege of Trieste in 1813.

5. Sir Henry Wyatt

Sir Henry Wyatt was a British statesman who lived in the 15th and 16th centuries. He was put into the Tower of London by King Richard III and placed in a cell with no bed and very little food. Richard's aim was that Sir Henry should die of 'natural causes' so that no one could blame him for the death. But the dastardly King's crafty plot was foiled. One night a cat came down the chimney into Sir Henry's cell and made friends with him, curling up on his chest to keep him warm. In the morning the cat disappeared; reappearing with a pigeon which it deposited by Sir Henry's side before leaving. When the jailer came he apologised that he was not allowed to bring more food. 'Will you cook this for me?' asked Sir Henry, holding up the pigeon. The jailer, having no idea how the pigeon had got into the cell and thinking it a miracle, said that he would. He took away the pigeon, prepared it, cooked it and returned it to Sir Henry. As the days went by the cat continued to take pigeons into the cell, the jailer continued to cook them and Sir Henry stayed alive, defying Richard III who was annoyed that his prisoner did not die. In the end Sir Henry outlived King Richard and was released from captivity by Henry VII. If Sir Henry hadn't been potty about cats before he was put in prison it's a pretty good bet that he was when he left. No one seems to know what happened to the cat but I like to think that Sir Henry took it home with him and ensured that it spent the rest of its life in unparalleled luxury.

6. Theodore Roosevelt

The former USA President Theodore Roosevelt had a six-toed grey cat called Slippers (named because of his large feet) who always made sure that he was the centre of attention. In 1906, the incorrigible Slippers blocked the entrance to a banqueting hall by the simple expedience of sprawling on the rug which lay in the middle of the doors into the room. The President, and his eminent guests were therefore obliged to walk around him. British Prime Minister Blair and his grinning wife would have doubtless had the cat removed and 'disappeared' to Isleworth. That was not Roosevelt's way. He loved the cat.

Slippers would often disappear from the White House for weeks on end but he always returned whenever a high level meeting was due to take place. Journalists recognised this and would keep an eye on the cat in order to know when major events at the White House were due to take place.

Roosevelt also had a cat called Tom Quartz (named after the cat in Mark Twain's book *Roughing It*) which was the subject of its own biography and was, indeed, the first, but no means the last, Presidential cat to claim such an honour.

7. Mohammed, the founder of Islam

Mohammed (who considered dogs unclean) had a cat called Muezza whom he adored. Mohammed was an extraordinarily sensible and well balanced fellow. Once, when he wanted to pray and the cat was sleeping on his sleeve, he simply cut the sleeve off rather than disturb the cat. In due course Mohammed gave a place in paradise to Muezza, and extended the privilege to all other cats.

It was Mohammed who stroked the cat's back three times to give it nine lives and the ability to land on its feet after a fall. It is also said that cats who have an M on their foreheads do so because of Mohammed's love of animals.

(There is, I should add, a competing theory that cats have an M on their foreheads because a cat approached Mary, the mother of Jesus, to be stroked shortly after the birth of Jesus. Mary, it is said, gently pushed the cat away, thereby putting an M on its forehead.)

8. Dr Albert Schweizer

Dr Albert Schweizer was a medical missionary famous for his work in Africa. Schweizer became ambidextrous in order to accommodate his cat.

Dr Schweizer, who won the Nobel Peace Prize in 1952, was left handed and when his cat Sizi fell asleep on his left arm (which she often did) Schweizer would write out prescriptions with his right hand.

Since doctors are notorious for having bad handwriting even when writing with their dominant hand this practice undoubtedly made life even more difficult for the local pharmacists.

9. Captain Lawrence Edward Grace Oates

Captain Oates was an English explorer who was a member of Captain Robert Scott's expedition which reached the South Pole in 1912. On the journey back from the Pole the explorers were delayed and weather-bound. Oates was so badly affected by frostbite that he became lame. Convinced that his disability would slow down his companions and affect their chances of reaching safety, Oates deliberately walked out of their tent into the blizzard knowing that he would die. When sacrificing his life so that his companions would have a better chance of survival Oates told other members of the Terra Nova Expedition to the Antarctic: 'I'm going outside. I may be some time.'

Less well known is the fact that it was the same Captain Oates who, when the explorers were leaving their supply ship, insisted that the expedition's cat Nigger be left on board when they set off for the Pole. A real English gentleman and cat lover.

10. Beryl Reid

Beryl Reid's life was saved by a cat during World War II. During the Blitz the cat would hide whenever a German plane came over but ignored British planes, thus enabling the English actress and comedienne to take cover whenever it was necessary. Beryl Reid had numerous cats (up to ten at a time) and their names included Cleopatra, Fred, Jenny, Billy, Clive, Elsie, Dimly, Sir Harry, Muriel, Ronnie, Emma and Georgie Girl. When Lulu, one of her cats, decided to live on the roof, Beryl Reid went up a ladder four times a day to feed her, thereby exhibiting a love of cats above and beyond the normal. Curiously, none of Miss Reid's cats liked fish.

Chapter Five

Seven Things To Do With A Cat

1. Stroke it.

2. Admire it.

3. Feed it.

4. Boast about it.

5. Let it in (or out).

6. Cuddle it.

7. Give it somewhere to sleep.

Chapter Six

Eighteen Favourite Proverbs Concerning Cats

Tracing the origins of proverbs is difficult. But I have, where possible, included the most likely country of origin.

1. Beware of people who dislike cats. (Ireland.)

2. In a cat's eye, all things belong to cats. (England.)

3. Cats, flies and women are ever at their toilets. (France.)

4. After dark all cats are leopards. (America.)

5. Honest as the cat when the meat is out of reach. (England.)

6. Happy owner, happy cat. Indifferent owner, reclusive cat. (China.)

7. The cat was created when the lion sneezed. (Arabia.)

8. A cat has nine lives. For three he plays, for three he strays and for the last three he stays. (England. In Shakespeare's *Romeo and Juliet*, Mercutio, incensed that Romeo refuses to stand up to his enemy Tybalt, himself picks a quarrel with Tybalt. When the challenged Tybalt asks, 'What would thou have with me?', Mercutio says: 'Good King of Cats, nothing but one of your nine lives.')

9. A cat's eyes are windows enabling us to see into another world. (Ireland.)

10. Happy is the home with at least one cat. (Italy.)

11. I gave an order to a cat, and the cat gave it to its tail. (China.)

12. Curiosity killed the cat, satisfaction brought it back. (England.)

13. When the cat's away the mice will play. (This version of the proverb originates in England. The French version is 'When the cat runs on the roofs, the mice dance on the floors.' The Italian version is: 'When the cat is not in the house, the mice will dance.' The unimaginative, rather stodgy German version is: 'The mouse reposes while the cat is outside the house.')

14. A cat is a lion in a jungle of small bushes. (India.)

15. A cat may look at a King. (England. The German version is: 'Even a cat may look at an Emperor'. The French variation is: 'Even a dog may look at a bishop.'

16. There are more ways of killing a cat than by choking it with cream. (England. Probably first used by Charles Kingsley in his novel *Westward Ho!*)

17. He's like a cat; fling him which way you will and he'll light on his legs. (England.)

18. Care killed a cat. (England. In *Much Ado About Nothing* Shakespeare writes: 'Though care killed a cat, thou hast mettle enough in thee to kill care.'

Tails of two kitties

Chapter Seven

Truly Heroic Cats
Seven Of The Bravest Cats Of All Time

Cats are braver and wiser than some Uprights might suspect. Here are just a few examples of how cats have proved their courage and good sense. This list is offered in no particular order. All these cats are brave and deserve a rousing three cheers, a standing ovation and a dish of the finest and freshest fish available. Several of these stories show that having a cat in the home can sometimes be even more useful than a smoke alarm. How many smoke alarms will bite you on the nose until you wake up?

1. When the small local post office belonging to her Upright was held up by an armed raider a cat called Lucky leaped over the counter and stuck her claws into the gunman. The gunman shrieked and fled in terror. Lucky was rewarded with a medal from the Postmaster General (though she would have probably preferred a nice fat juicy mouse).

2. Plucky tortoiseshell Scarlett didn't hesitate when she saw that the garage was on fire. Scarlett knew that her four-week-old kittens were still inside the garage. She darted into the flames five times. And five times she came out carefully holding a terrified kitten in her mouth. After each brave mission of mercy she put the rescued kitten down on the kerb across the street before darting back into

the flames to fetch the next one. By the time Scarlett had rescued all her kittens the smoke was so bad she could hardly see – so she counted her kittens up by touching them in turn with her nose. Only when she was content that all five of her kittens were safe, did Scarlett let rescuers take her and her family to a local animal shelter for treatment.

3. A two-year-old cat called Coffee was dozing quietly in the kitchen when he noticed that the chip pan was on fire. Coffee, realising that something needed to be done quickly, leapt into action. He gently bit his dozing Upright on the nose and butted him until he woke up and put out the fire. The weary but lucky houseowner, who had dropped off for forty winks with the chip pan on a lit stove, was saved.

4. When he saw a nervous kitten run into the middle of a busy road and get struck by a car, a courageous ginger tom cat called Biffy ignored his own safety and darted to the rescue. Having abandoned the comparative safety of the pavement he weaved in and out of the cars and dragged the wounded kitten to safety.

5. Fire on board a ship can quickly become a real emergency. When a fire broke out in the galley on an American trawler the boat was soon alight – and the danger was spreading fast. Smoke poured into the cabin where the trawler's captain was fast asleep. Disregarding the danger to herself the ship's mascot, a brave cat called Lizzie, jumped through the smoke and flames and clawed at the captain until he woke up. After the fire was put out both Lizzie and the captain were saved.

6. A ginger cat called Tiddles was sleeping downstairs when he suddenly realised that the house was on fire. He had only moved in recently and he wasn't about to see his new home and his new Uprights destroyed by flames. Tiddles ran upstairs, sat on the chest of the sleeping male Upright, miaowed loudly and tapped the man on the head until he woke up. Tiddles and the two Uprights were all saved.

7.   A Persian Blue called Jasmin and her Upright were fast asleep when
     an electrical fire started in a downstairs room. Jasmin went down
     to investigate and found herself trapped. She screamed loudly until
     she woke her sleeping Upright. The Upright managed to escape
     through a bedroom window and get help. Jasmin was rescued by
     the Fire Brigade.

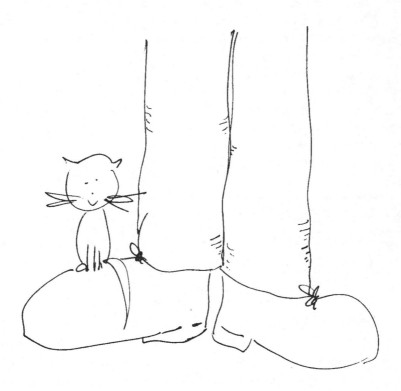

Chapter Eight

Why Do Cats Climb Trees?

Why do cats climb trees? Is it to explore the outer edges of their capability to withstand awesome trials and tribulations? Is it to investigate the unexplored reaches of our wonderful world? Is it to display their skills and to impress their peers? Do they climb to get nearer to the stars? Is it because they want to get in touch with their spiritual side by venturing into the silence that can be found only at the top of a tall tree?

To answer this vital question I interviewed a number of cats and then, with the aid of a specially designed computer program, and teams of highly trained software engineers, converted their answers into the table that appears below, published here for the very first time.

1. There are no dogs up trees.

2. The noises motorcycles make are less audible up trees.

3. There are no children up trees (not high up anyway).

4. When you go up higher there are no dogs and you can't even hear any dogs.

5. The trees are there waiting to be climbed.

6. The noises the dustmen make are less noticeable up trees.

7. When you get really high there are definitely no dogs, you can't hear any dogs and, if you close your eyes and look upwards, you won't even see any dogs. No wonder they say that heaven is high up in the sky.

8. You can pretend not to hear Uprights calling if you don't want to do whatever it is they want you to do (or not do).

9. If you have done something bad (broken a vase, for example) and you go up a tree and pretend to get stuck the Uprights will be so worried about you that they will forget about whatever it is that you have done (broken a vase, for example). When you come down, instead of shouting at you, they will give you breast of chicken and fresh cream.

10. After you've been up a tree for a while you can convince yourself that dogs don't exist.

The cuddle

Chapter Nine

Odd Relationships Between Cats And Other Animals

1. In North Thailand a two-year-old black and white cat has become best friends with a field mouse who used to live in a nearby paddy field. The cat quite happily shares her milk bowl with the field mouse. After meals she bathes the mouse with her tongue and lets it cuddle up in her fur to sleep.

2. When a cat who'd been out hunting arrived home he had an unusual present in his mouth: a live baby grey squirrel. The baby squirrel was immediately adopted by another cat who was feeding her own kittens at the time. The squirrel quickly settled in, was fed along with the other kittens and treated by the mother cat as though she was one of her own kittens.

3. In Lincolnshire, a blackbird regularly gets into a house through the cat-flap and eats food which has been put out for the two resident cats. Amazingly the two cats don't complain but just watch the bird from their nearby beds.

4. When an owlet was abandoned by her mother she was adopted by a kindly cat and treated as though she was one of the cat's own kittens. The kittens and the owl played games and slept together.

5. A feral Scottish wildcat lives and sleeps with a pet white rat. The cat spits and scratches at Uprights but is very loving to the rat who

pulls the cat's tail around him like a shawl when he wants to go to sleep.

6.   After a two-month-old grey tabby kitten was abandoned by her mother a one-year-old lurcher-retriever decided to play mother. Within two days the dog was lactating and suckling the kitten.

7.   A black and white cat who lives in London sleeps in a heated glass tortoise tank with his head resting on the shell of the resident tortoise.

"Here is the mews."

Chapter Ten

A Visit To Vernon Coleman's Catland

Mrs Harvester-Brown's students didn't use books for their deportment classes, but the results were every bit as good.

A pigeon among the cats

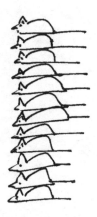 

Kitty liked birthdays. She didn't mind whether or not her presents were wrapped, as long as she got a lot of them. To her, quantity was of paramount importance.

Small is beautiful

Russian cats.

"Will one of you please answer that cat?"

Cats they knew sometimes referred to them as the odd couple, but they were very happy together and to them that was all that seemed important.

*Ginger and Fluffy still felt they needed to supervise little Tigger
when he did his homework.*

People always seem to know that we're related," said Jeffery and Lionel. "But we don't know how they can tell. Personally, we can't see any similarity at all."

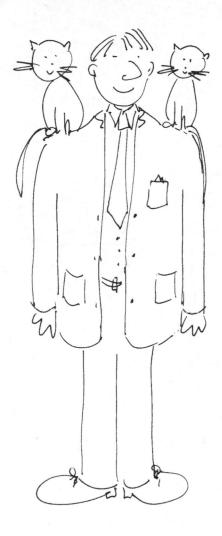

Everyone who knew him said that
Albert was a very well-balanced person.

When Mrs Dubble-Barol went shopping she always carried her cat Matilda with her. This meant that she had to hire a man (in a smart uniform) to walk behind her carrying the packets and parcels she'd bought.

"Do you think we should stop giving Sooty his vitamin supplement?
He's nearly three months old now."

*When Seraphina went for a walk she always felt safe
(and never even knew when it rained).*

The cat sat on the Matt

Matt sat on the cat

"But it <u>looks</u> like a mouse," said Peter.
"Just because it <u>looks</u> like a mouse doesn't mean it <u>is</u> a mouse," said Tiger, gravely.

Thin woman: "I've heard it said that some people get to look like their cats. Isn't that the stupidest thing you ever heard?"
Fat woman: "Oh absolutely. What fools some folk are."

For some reason, the kittens felt safe when Tiger was around.

"We have to have two cats," said Myrtle,
"to stop our books falling off the mantelpiece."

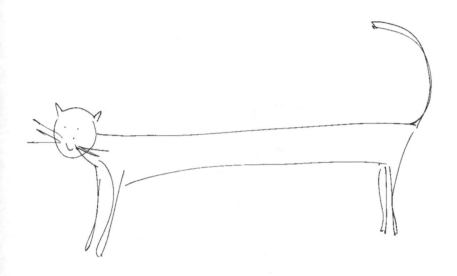

The Stretch Cat – bred for very posh occasions and known to cat breeders and experts as Felix Limousini.

*It is, of course, nonsense to say that cats ever
look or behave like their Uprights.*

"And the most important thing to remember is this: No matter what you've done wrong, always make it look like the dog did it."

All cats like being the focus of attention.

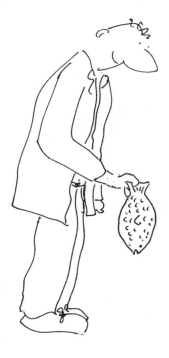

*"It looks very nice. Do you think I could have it lightly poached with
roasted almonds and a slice of lemon? And, perhaps, a tossed green
salad and a saucer of white Bordeaux slightly chilled?"*

When Sparky first caught sight of his tail he was confused. He didn't know what to make of it. Then the tail moved. Alarmed, Sparky ran away. When he finally stopped running he turned round and was astonished to see that the tail had followed him. Everywhere he went the tail came after him. Eventually, Sparky turned round and stared hard at the tail. "Oh well," he said to himself "if it's that keen to be with me it must like me a lot." Tentatively, he licked the tail. The tail twitched. Sparky licked it again. "Would you like to be my friend?" he asked. The tail twitched. "That's nice," said Sparky. "I've never had a friend before."

The Four Mousekateers

"I know we are running away," said Bertie. "But if we are running away from everything, where are we going?"

*Tommy loved his young Upright but,
nevertheless, sometimes wished that his
entrepreneurial instincts were not quite so
well-developed.*

Le Chat Show

"Am I right in thinking that you are the cats who have been bullying my sister Kitty?"

"I can't quite remember why I came up here. I don't like it. Would someone please help me down?"

Aunt Maud liked Perry, her 12-year-old cat, very much indeed but
sometimes felt that the cat had grown too big to be sitting on her lap.
"I should be sitting on <u>his</u> lap – if he had one," she told everyone who
would listen.

Samson loved his little Upright, Delilah. He gave her a lovely basket and regular meals three times a day.

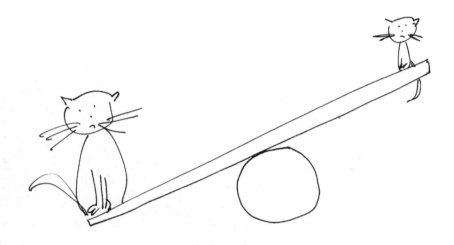

"This see-saw doesn't work," said the kitten, sadly.
"I think it must be broken."

Chauncey was definitely a two-lap cat.

The first Parent-Teachers meeting was a great success

Teacher: "When I say your first name just say 'Prrrr, Miss' ... Ready?"
Kittens: "Yes, Miss!"

Doctor: "Stroke this cat three times a day and for ten minutes before bedtime. Your troubles will not disappear but they will seem far less important."

Oscar hated fireworks, so his Upright always wore a
long dress on November 5th.

American Cat

French Cat

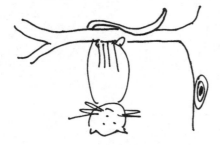

Australian Cat

Swiss cat
(with fish bank)

The leaning cat of Pisa was every bit as remarkable as they had heard.

Chapter Eleven

Eleven Ways To Keep Your Cat Alive And Healthy

1. Road traffic accidents are the most common cause of death or serious injury to cats. The motor car kills far more cats than dogs – or any natural predator. Cats who move from a quiet area to a home near to a busy road are particularly at risk but even cats who grow up near to a busy road can still be vulnerable. It is always good to be able to allow a cat the freedom to roam around outside, but if you live in a built up area with busy roads nearby it will almost certainly extend your cat's life expectation if you keep him or her indoors. It is almost impossible to cat-proof a garden so that you can prevent your cat attempting to cross a busy road. Cats are most at danger when they leave the house at night. That is when they are most likely to be hit by drunken motorists speeding home on the wrong side of the road (or, indeed, attacked by predators such as feral cats or dogs roaming free). Don't turn your cat out of the house at night – unless he or she really wants to go and is genuinely unhappy about staying indoors.

2. An adult cat may survive a fall of up to about 20 feet without injury, but a fall of any greater height is likely to result in serious damage. If you live in an apartment which is higher than that it would be wise either to keep your windows closed or to fit cat-proof bars to the windows. It is possible to purchase bars which can be easily put into place and then removed if you wish to open

a window. All too often a cat will find the attraction of passing birds irresistible and will climb out onto a windowsill. From the windowsill it is too often just one small slip to oblivion. Cats always like to think of themselves as unerringly sure-footed but it is known (very occasionally, of course) for a cat to slip, be distracted or misjudge a jump.

3.   On moving to a new home, cats should be kept indoors for a few days until they have overcome the stress of the move and have realised that, despite the new surroundings, the life of the family is going on much as before. Cats will be far more capable of adapting to their new surroundings, and finding their way back to their new home, if they have been allowed time to adjust. Putting butter on a cat's feet forces the cat to lick itself and has the effect of calming it down. Cats will normally only clean themselves when they are feeling secure so cleaning itself makes a cat feel secure. Clever stuff, eh?

4.   The majority of cats sustain minor wounds occasionally. Wounds may be a result of a fight with a dog or another cat or may be a result of a battle with an animal the cat was hoping to turn into food. My much loved cat Alice (the internationally acclaimed author of 'Alice's Diary' and 'Alice's Adventures') was, in her all too short life, bitten by a mouse, a rat and a squirrel (though not all at once). At various times in her life she also tangled with a fox, a rabbit, a bat, a lizard, a buzzard and a shrew. The shrew bit her on the nose and drew blood – much to Alice's disgust and shame. The ears, face and front paws are the parts of a cat most commonly attacked. Alice isn't the only cat I've known to be bitten on the nose by a shrew or vole fighting for its life. It is always wise to get a veterinary surgeon to see a cat who has been injured though emergency care may be needed before the cat can be taken to a vet. For example, if a cat has been severely wounded, and is losing blood, the blood flow should be stopped or slowed down by using simple finger pressure.

5.   Kittens find wires and electricity cables strangely attractive. In their uneducated enthusiasm they are quite likely to bite through the wires. Biting through electrical wiring is even more dangerous than running

across a busy road and is usually immediately fatal. Even if it isn't fatal the cat will use up at least one of its lives and sustain substantial electrical burns to his or her mouth and paws. (Whether it is alive or dead, if a kitten or cat is found next to a bitten-into wire, the first step must be to isolate the current by removing the plug from the socket and/or switching off the electricity at the mains. It won't help your cat if you get electrocuted too. Don't touch a cat which is, or even may be, in contact with a live wire.)

6. Cats, especially long-haired cats, are vulnerable to heat stroke. A cat will normally find a shady corner where it can hide away from the heat but cats are particularly likely to be vulnerable when travelling in a cage or in a car. If you are travelling with a cat make sure that he or she has plenty of water to drink and check regularly to make sure that all is well.

7. Cartoonists often depict cats trapped on roofs or at the top of trees. It is, for some reason, something which they find amusing. In fact, cats (well, older ones anyway) are usually wise enough to avoid getting into positions from which they cannot extricate themselves. When a cat does get stuck it is usually because it is involved in some sort of chase (either as the chaser or the chasee) and has thrown all caution and good sense to the wind. Alice once got stuck sitting on a chimney pot. She had run up onto the roof to escape noisy builders (this was back in the days when workmen could be persuaded to turn up and do things) and was so frozen with fear that she refused all inducements to come down and steadfastly clung to the chimney pot. Eventually, a workman volunteered to climb up a long ladder and crawl onto the roof. When he got near her, Alice ran back down the roof before leaping into my waiting arms. Using a decoy would-be rescuer isn't something I recommend but it worked for me. (The workman was so shaken by the incident that he spent the rest of the day lying down being treated with cups of tea and slices of cake.) The only way to avoid this problem completely is to live in a tent. It is my experience that cats will not climb onto tent roofs.

8. Cats are very susceptible to respiratory problems. The smoke from fires, cigarettes or burning toast can be very distressing for cats and

may cause severe respiratory problems – so take care.

9. Uprights should groom their cats – however fastidious each cat may seem to be. Grooming can reveal parasites which the cat cannot remove. Cats like being groomed and regard it as a sign of real friendship. I've been groomed by several of the cats who have shared my life and have always regarded it as a great honour. A jet black male cat called Dick used to groom my hair and would sit clinging to my shoulder and neck for ages licking and checking my scalp for unwanted parasites. The raspy licking tickled a bit to begin with but once I'd got used to it, I found it a pleasant and relaxing experience.

10. A traditional way to diagnose illness in a cat is to check its nose. If the nose is cold and noticeably wet, then the cat may have a chill, cold or even cat flu.

11. A cat's digestive system is ill-equipped to cope with poisons. Unfortunately, cats tend to be blessed with rather more than their fair share of curiosity and as a result often taste or eat things which are bad for them. Cats may get poisoned through their habit of eating mice and other small creatures. If a mouse has been poisoned and the cat eats the mouse there is a very good chance that the cat will be poisoned too. So, don't allow anyone to put rat or mouse poison down anywhere that your cat is likely to roam. (I don't approve of such poisons whether there is a cat around or not.) And don't use poisons in your garden if the garden is shared by a cat. A cat who eats poisoned weeds or grass may become severely ill or die.

The three terrors

Chapter Twelve

What To Call A Cat

There is absolutely nothing wrong with calling a cat Smokey, Blackie, Sooty or Tiddles as long as the name has been decided on after some consideration – rather than selected at random, after no more than a moment's thought. Choosing a name for a cat is just as important as choosing a name for a baby. It's a task which requires a great deal of thought and yet so many Uprights just settle for the first name that comes into their heads.

To help the selection process I have prepared two lists of some of the prettiest names I can think of for cats – all of these names proved popular when tried out on a random selection of cats. (There are, of course, hundreds if not thousands, of other equally wonderful names for cats.)

In my book *The Cat's Own Annual* I pointed out that although some cats are fussy about their name most cats don't much mind what they get called as long the calling is done politely and respectfully.

I also pointed out that the choice of name might be important if you are likely to spend a lot of time calling your cat and expecting him or her to respond. Cats have very good hearing (a cat's hearing stops at around 65 kilohertz whereas human hearing stops at 20 kilohertz) but through a quirk of fate which I don't begin to understand most cats respond most readily to names that end in an 'ee' sound. Call your cat `Billy', `Julie', `Tommy', `Smokey', `Sooty' or `Blackie' and he or she will respond perfectly well. But to a cat names such as `Cuthbert' and

`Doris' don't just sound like proper cat names. Stand in the garden yelling `Prince Alfred of Transylvania the IVth' and the cat who is supposed to be responding may simply think that you're clearing your throat or are having some sort of seizure.

With a typically cavalier toss of the head in the direction of political correctness I've prepared one list for female cats and one list for male cats.

Names for female cats:

Aisha	Dixie	Lucy
Alice	Dottatina	Matilda
Aloisha	Dottie	Melissa
Annabelle	Emma	Odelia
Arabella	Flower	Prunella
Ayala	Fluffy	Rainbow
Beatrice	Giselle	Sally
Cerys	Holly	Sapphire
Chantelle	Honey	Sephratina
Chika	Kitty	Tammy
Chloe	Layla	Tiddlelina
Colette	Lizzie	Thomasina
Coral	Lucky	Trilby

My Fur Lady

Names for male cats:

Alfie	Hector	Sammy
Blackie	Herbie	Smokey
Carey	Jack	Socrates
Chauncey	Jackson	Sooty
Danny	Jethro	Sparky
Dick	Julius	Tiddles
Dickie	Leroy	Tiger
Dougie	Marmaduke	Tigger
Dudley	Marmalade	Timmy
Eddie	Merlin	Toby
Elvis	Otis	Tom
Ginger	Percy	Tommy
Harley	Rana	Tully
Harry	Robbie	Vincent
Harvey	Rocky	Voltaire
Heathcliffe	Sam	Whitby

You called?

Chapter Thirteen

The Things People Say About Cats

'What greater gift than the love of a cat?'

Charles Dickens

'I learnt the lesson of life from a little kitten of mine, one of two. The old cat comes in and says, very cross: 'I didn't ask you in here. I like to have my Missus to myself.' And he runs at them. The bigger and handsome kitten runs away, but the littler one stands her ground, and when the old enemy comes near enough kisses his nose, and makes the peace. That is the lesson of life, to kiss one's enemy's nose, always standing one's ground.'

Florence Nightingale

'A cat's got her own opinion of human beings. She don't say much, but you can tell enough to make you anxious not to hear the whole of it.'

Jerome K. Jerome

'Whosoever tortures animals has no soul, and the good spirit of the God is not in him. Even should he look deep inside himself, one can never trust him.'

Johann Wolfgang von Goethe

'Only skin deep lies the feral nature of the cat, unchanged still. I just had the misfortune to rock on to our cat's leg, as she was lying playfully spread out under my chair. Imagine the sound that arose, and which was excusable; but what will you say to the fierce growls and flashing eyes with which she met me for a quarter of an hour thereafter? No tiger in its jungle could have been savager.'

Henry David Thoreau

'You own a dog but you feed a cat.'

Jenny de Vries

'The cat does not offer services. The cat offers itself. Of course he wants care and shelter. You don't buy love for nothing. Like all pure creatures, cats are practical.'

William S. Burroughs

'Civilisation is defined by the presence of cats.'

Anonymous

'Cats do not have to be shown how to have a good time, for they are unfailingly ingenious in that respect.'

James Mason

'Careful observers may foretell the hour
(By sure prognostics) when to dread a shower
While rain depends, the pensive cat gives o'er
Her frolics, and pursues her tail no more.'

Jonathan Swift

'I've met many thinkers and many cats, but the wisdom of cats is infinitely superior.'

Hippolyte Taine

'If a dog jumps into your lap, it is because he is fond of you; but if a cat does the same thing, it is because your lap is warmer.'

A. N. Whitehead

Dottie loved her kitten very much and didn't in the slightest bit mind that it had grown rather larger than is considered 'normal' in cat-fancying circles

'How we behave towards cats here below determines our status in heaven.'

Robert A. Heinlein

'If you want to know the character of a man, find out what his cat thinks of him.'

Anonymous

'Watch a cat when it enters a room for the first time. It searches and smells about, it is not quiet for a moment, it trusts nothing until it has examined and made acquaintance with everything.'

Jean-Jacques Rousseau

'Cats can be very funny, and have the oddest ways of showing they're glad to see you. Rudimace always peed in our shoes.'

W. H. Auden

'There are two means of refuge from the miseries of life: music and cats.'

Albert Schweitzer

'When my cat and I entertain each other with mutual apish tricks, as playing with a garter, who knows but that I make my cat more sport than she makes me? Shall I conclude her to be simple, that has her time to begin or refuse to play as freely as I myself have? Nay, who knows but that it is a defect of my not understanding her language (for doubtless cats talk and reason with one another) that we agree no better? And who knows but that she pities me for being no wiser than to play with her, and laughs and censures my folly for making sport for her, when we two play together.'

Michel de Montaigne

'No matter how much cats fight, there always seem to be plenty of kittens.'

Abraham Lincoln

'Thousands of years ago, cats were worshipped as gods. Cats have never forgotten this.'

Anonymous

'To respect a cat is the beginning of the aesthetic sense.'

Erasmus Darwin

'By associating with the cat, one only risks becoming richer.'

Colette

'A kitten is in the animal world what a rosebud is in the garden.'

Robert Southey

'Miaow is like aloha – it can mean anything.'

Hank Ketchum

'It is easy to understand why the rabble dislike cats. A cat is beautiful, it suggests ideas of luxury, cleanliness, voluptuous pleasures.'

Charles Baudelaire

'Even overweight cats instinctively know the cardinal rule: when fat, arrange yourself in slim poses.'

John Weitz

'If you want to be a psychological novelist and write about human beings the best thing you can do is to keep a pair of cats.'

Aldous Huxley

'Someone once said that a dog looked up to man as its superior, but a horse regarded a man as its equal, and that a cat looked down on him as its inferior.'

Sir Compton Mackenzie

'A cat has absolute emotional honesty: human beings, for one reason or another, may hide their feelings, but a cat does not.'

Ernest Hemingway

'I cannot imagine a pleasant retired life of peace and medication without a cat in the house.'

Paul von Hindenburg

'A kitten is so flexible that she is almost double; the hind parts are equivalent to another kitten with which the forepart plays. She does not discover that her tail belongs to her till you tread upon it.'

Henry David Thoreau

'Even the stupidest cat seems to know more than any dog.'

Eleanor Clark

'A cat is there when you call her – if she doesn't have something better to do.'

Bill Adler

'The cat could very well be man's best friend but would never stoop to admitting it.'

Doug Larson

'People that hate cats will come back as mice in their next life.'

Faith Resnick

'If I die before my cat, I want a little of my ashes put in his food so I can live inside him.'

Drew Barrymore

'Way down deep we are all motivated by the same urges. Cats have the courage to live by them.'

Jim Davis

'There are many intelligent species in the universe. They are all owned by cats.'

Anonymous

'A small pet is often an excellent companion for the sick, for long chronic cases especially.'

Florence Nightingale

'As anyone who has ever been around a cat for any length of time well knows cats have enormous patience with the limitations of the human mind.'

Cleveland Amory

'If it's raining at the back door, every cat is convinced there's a good chance that it won't be raining at the front door.'

William Toms

'Women and cats will do as they please, and men and dogs should relax and get used to the idea.'

Robert A Heinlein

'For me, one of the pleasures of cats' company is their devotion to bodily comfort.'

Sir Compton Mackenzie

'In the beginning, God created man, but seeing him so feeble, He gave him the cat.'

Warren Eckstein

The cat who had had the cream.

Chapter Fourteen

The Twelve Words People Use Most When Describing Cats

1. Cuddly

2. Fluffy

3. Adorable

4. Soft

5. Graceful

6. Supple

7. Aloof

8. Loveable

9. Warm

10. Independent

11. Comforting

12. Elegant

Chapter Fifteen

Famous People And The (Sometimes Surprising) Names They Gave Their Cats

ALBERT SCHWEITZER: Sizi

ALEXANDER DUMAS: Mysouff

ANATOLE FRANCE: Hamilcar

ANDY WARHOL: Hester: Tuppence

B. KLIBAN: Nitty

BARBARA HEPWORTH: Mimi, Nicholas, Tobey

BEAU BRUMMELL: Angolina

BERYL REID: Billy, Cleopatra, Clive, Dimly, Elsie, Emma, Fred, Georgie Girl, Jenny, Lulu, Muriel, Ronnie, Sir Harry

CALVIN COOLIDGE: Blackie, Tiger, Timmie

CARDINAL RICHELIEU: Gazette, Lucifer, Ludovic the Cruel, Perruque, Pyramus, Racan, Rita, Rubis, Serpolet, Soumise, Thisbe

CHARLES DICKENS: The Master's Cat, William (later renamed Williamina)

CHARLOTTE BRONTË: Tiger, Tom

CHRISTINA ROSSETTI: Grimalkin

CLAUDE DEBUSSY: Line

CLEOPATRA: Charmian

COLETTE: Ba-tou, Chad, Chartreux, Fanchette, Kapok, Kiki-La-Doucette, Kro, La Toutea, La Chatte, Minionne, Muscat, La Chatte Dernière, Petitea, Pinichette, Toune, Zwerg

COMPTON MACKENZIE: Pippo, Sylvia, Tootoose

DANTE GABRIEL ROSSETTI: Zoe

DOROTHY L SAYERS: Timothy

DUSTY SPRINGFIELD: Nicholas Alexis, Malaysia

EDGAR ALLAN POE: Caterina

EDITH SITWELL: Belkaer, Leo, Orion, Shadow

ERASMUS DARWIN: Persian Snow

ERNEST HEMINGWAY: Alley Cat, Barbershop, Bigotes, Christian, Christopher Columbus, Crazy, Dillinger, Ecstasy, F.Puss, Fats, Friendless Brother, Furhouse, Thruster, Willy

F. SCOTT FITZGERALD: Chopin

FLORENCE NIGHTINGALE: Bismarck, Disraeli, Gladstone (and 57 others)

FRANCES HODGSON BURNETT: Dick, Dorah

GEORGES CLEMENCEAU: Prudence

HAROLD ROSS: Missus

HAROLD WILSON: Nemo

HENRY DAVID THOREAU: Min

H. G. WELLS: Mr Peter Wells

HIPPOLYTE TAIRE: Ebene, Mitonne, Puss

JACK KEROUAC: Tuffy

JAMES DEAN: Marcus

JAMES MASON: Flower Face, Folly, Lady Leeds, Sadie, Topboy,Tree, Whitey

JEROME K. JEROME: Tittums

JOHN CHEEVER: Delmone Schwartz

KINGSLEY AMIS: Saran Snow

LOUIS WAIN: Peter (later known as Peter the Great)

LOUIS XV: Collegue

LYTTON STRACHEY: Tiberius

MARK TWAIN: Amanda, Annanna, Apollinaris, Babylon, Beezlebub, Billiards, Blatherskite, Buffalo Bill, Danbury, Sindbad, Sour Mash, Stan,

Stray Kit, Tammary, Zoroaster *(Mark Twain deliberately gave his cats difficult names in order to teach his children how to pronounce difficult words.)*

MAX BEERBOHM: Stretchi

MICHEL DE MONTAIGNE: Madame Vanity

PATRICIA HIGHSMITH: Spider

PAUL GALLICO: Chin Chilla

PAUL KLEE: Bimbo, Fritzi, Mys, Nuggi

P. G. WODEHOUSE: Poona

RALPH VAUGHAN WILLIAMS: Crispin, Friskin

RAYMOND CHANDLER: Taki

RENE DESCARTES: Monsieur Grat

ROBERT SOUTHEY: Baron Raticide Waouhler, Bona Marietta, Bona Fidelia, Earl Tomlemange, His Serene Highness the Archduke Rumpelstilzchen, Marquis Macburn, Hurlyburlybuss, Lord Nelson, Madame Bianchi, Pulcheria, Skaratsch, Sir Thomas Dido, The Zombi

TALLULA BANKHEAD: Dolly

THOMAS CARLYLE: Columbine

THOMAS HARDY: Cobby

T. S. ELIOT: Pettipaws, George Pushdragon, Wiscus

VAN HEFLIN: Mousetrap, Silk hat

VICTOR HUGO: Chanoine, Gavroche

VIRGINA WOOLF: Potto

VIVIEN LEIGH: Boy, Nichols, Poo Jones

W. H. DAVIES: Venus

W. H. AUDEN: Rudimace Leonora

WINSTON CHURCHILL: Jock, Nelson

When Marmaduke met Beatrice it was love at first sight.

Chapter Sixteen

The Most Common Superstitions Involving Cats

(The country from which each superstition originated is given in brackets.)

1. If you are at home and the cat who shares your house starts to wash behind its ears then you may expect visitors. (Holland).

2. If you hear a cat sneeze it is good luck. Everyone who hears the sneeze will share in the good luck. (Italy).

3. When you move to a new home you should put your cat into your home through a window rather than through a door. This will ensure that the cat never runs away. (America. Presumably dating back prior to the building of high rise apartment buildings. It might be tricky to put a cat through a sealed window on the 16th floor of a tower block.)

4. If you dream of a white cat then you have good luck coming. (America.)

5. A cat washing behind its ears is a sign that it will rain soon. (England. Given the weather in England this seems likely to be one of the most accurate of all feline predictors.)

6. It is bad luck to cross a stream while carrying a cat. (France. I doubt if you will find yourself crossing streams while carrying cats on a daily basis but if you do find yourself tempted remember this superstition. Only once can I remember carrying a cat across a

stream myself. Alice once waded through a stream because she had spotted me on the opposite bank. When she had finished wading she spent several minutes shaking each leg in turn. When I returned across the stream I picked her up and carried her.)

7. If you see a cat sleeping with all its four paws tucked underneath its body you can safely assume that there is cold weather ahead. (England.)

8. If you spot a one-eyed cat, spit on your thumb, rub the spittle into the palm of your hand and make a wish. Your wish will come true. (America.)

9. If you spot a strange black cat on your porch you are assured of good times ahead. (Scotland.)

10. You will always be lucky if you know how to make friends with strange cats. (England.)

LuLu looked everywhere for her kitten but just couldn't find him.

Chapter Seventeen

A Bunch Of Strange Cat Tales

When novelist Thomas Hardy died his body was supposed to have been buried in Stinsford Churchyard in Dorset. But there is a story that his sister's cat stole the great author's heart from the kitchen table before it could be buried. Just why and how Mr Hardy's heart got separated from the rest of his body is not something I want to go into.

Nobel prize winning French novelist Anatole France had a cat called Hamilcar who acted more like a wife than a cat. When Hamilcar decided that it was time for bed he would knock Anatole's pen from his hand. Charles Dickens had a similar problem. One of his cats, called The Master's Cat, used to snuff out Dickens's candle when he decided that The Master had done enough for the day. Without The Master's Cat controlling the candle Dickens might well have given us *Pickwick Papers Parts II and III.*

Thriller writer Raymond Chandler had a cat called Taki who was very good at catching animals. However, either through rank incompetence or a gentle heart, Taki never actually killed any of the creatures she caught. Instead she took everything she caught into the house and presented it to Chandler who then took it back outside and released it into the wild.

Doubtless many small animals made the trip on numerous occasions.

I'm sure other cats do this too though it is, I suspect, rare for a cat always to refuse to eat what it catches.

My dear Alice used to bring animals into the house and let them go. Sometimes she would bring in a mouse and drop it at my feet as a present. She would then get slightly peeved when I failed to eat the proffered gift and distinctly offended when I took it out into the garden and let it go.

I remember that one summer Alice brought in a lizard from the garden so many times that the lizard and I became quite close chums. Alice would bring the lizard into the kitchen, let it go and then watch it slither and wriggle around until it managed to slide underneath some piece of furniture. She would then lose interest in the lizard and leave it to me to catch and take back to what I hoped and believed was its home in a dry stone wall. On an early journey into the kitchen the lizard lost most of its tail and Alice was absolutely fascinated by the way that while the lizard slithered one way its tail set off in a completely different direction. This flummoxed Alice, as, of course, it was meant to do. She didn't know whether to chase the lizard or its tail and sat, transfixed, looking first at one and then at the other, for the all the world like a matronly figure comfortably watching the tennis at Wimbledon. The tail grew back in due course but in the period while the lizard was without the majority of its wiggly bit (I'm afraid I christened the unfortunate lizard 'Stumpy') Alice seemed constantly rather disappointed that it didn't do its party trick and divide into two.

She usually ate everything she caught except for bats, which always rather confused her, and, of course, for voles and shrews which she considered only good for catching and certainly no good at all for eating, so I rather suspect that after an initial, exploratory taste of the separated tail she had found the lizard rather too rich for her taste.

French literary superstar Alexander Dumas, author of *The Three Musketeers*, had a cat called Mysouff. Early in his career Dumas worked as a clerk for the Duke of Orleans and would set off for work every morning at 9.30am with Mysouff faithfully following behind. The cat would stop when he decided he had gone far enough from home and would sit patiently and wait for Dumas to come back. At 5.30 pm, as Dumas returned home the cat would be waiting and would complete the return journey behind his master. If for any reason Dumas was held up the cat would not wait but would just make his way back home alone.

During the Second World War Winston Churchill was in bed with flu when a Minister entered his bedroom and looked rather disapprovingly at the fact that Churchill's cat Nelson (a huge black cat whom the great Statesman adored) was purring on his feet. 'This cat does more for the war effort than you do,' said Churchill in defence of his feline friend. 'He acts as a hot water bottle and saves the nation fuel and power.'

When Ramsey MacDonald was a young man he worked at a London Post Office where a cat had been trained to lick stamps. For good luck MacDonald got the cat to lick the stamp he wanted to put on a letter he was sending to the Times. The letter was duly published and MacDonald's political career was started. MacDonald eventually became Prime Minister and later credited the cat with having launched his career.

Chopin's *Waltz No 3 in F Major* was inspired when a cat walked across the keys of Chopin's piano. Similarly, Domenico Scarlatti's *Cat Fugue* was inspired by the sounds produced when his pet cat Pulcinella walked over the keys of his harpsichord.

Early film star and comedian Mack Sennett was the first person to put a cat in a film. A grey stray appeared on the set one day when Sennett was filming. Instead of throwing a tantrum and having the cat removed from the set Sennett made the cat a part of the scene. He called her Pepper and she subsequently starred in other films. Pepper is believed to have been the only cat ever to appear in silent films.

Because there wasn't any cat litter available Anne Frank's cat Mouschi peed on the floor in the loft where the famous diarist and her family were hiding. The cat's pee dripped onto a barrel of potatoes which stank so much they had to be thrown out. It might not sound much now but when it happened this was something of a disaster for everyone concerned. (Except for Mouschi, of course. The cat probably blamed the dog the Frank family didn't have.)

Jerome K. Jerome, English author of one of the funniest books ever written, the classic *Three Men in a Boat*, owned a cat whose brain had, in Jerome's own words, 'run entirely to motherliness'. The cat brought up an orphaned spaniel puppy and a squirrel as her own. She boxed the dog's ears if it dared to bark. She also held down the squirrel's bushy tail with her paws and licked it constantly to try and make it flat like a cat's tail. Sadly, for Jerome's maternal cat, the squirrel's tail simply could not be trained – it just flicked up over the squirrel's head again every time the cat let it go.

When English artist David Hockney painted Ossie Clark and his wife Celia together he included their white cat Blanche in the painting. For reasons known only to himself Mr Hockney called the painting: *Mr and Mrs Clark and Percy*.

The French born painter Balthus, whose real name was Count Balthaser Klossowski de Rola, found a stray tom cat when he was just ten years old. He took the cat home on a journey which involved travel by both boat and tram and called him Mitsou. Later, Balthus used to take the cat for walks on a lead.

French painter Jean Auguste Dominique Ingres was preparing to be presented to Prince Borghese when he heard that his cat Patrocle had died. Ingres cancelled his appointment and spent the rest of the day in mourning.

Art world superstar Leonardo da Vinci once painted a portrait of the infant Jesus with his mother and included a cat in the painting. He called the painting: 'Madonna and Child with a Cat'.

Just before British racing driver John Cobb set off to the USA to break the land speed record two kittens were born in the cockpit of the car Cobb was due to drive. Cobb called the kittens Inlet and Exhaust.

There has been a cat living at the British Prime Minister's Residence in London for many years. The Royal Society for the Prevention of Cruelty to Animals gave Number 10 Downing Street a white, black and tabby cat called Wilberforce who remained in post throughout the reigns of Prime Ministers Wilson, Heath, Callaghan and Thatcher and who was duly followed by a cat called Humphrey. The years of tradition ended when the Blairs entered No 10. The Blairs immediately got rid of the resident cat. Attempts were made by the Prime Minister's spin doctors to convince cat lovers that the cat had merely been 'retired' but there were some suspicions about the fate of the missing cat. Humphrey was eventually produced and was said to be living quietly in the suburbs but the cat who was produced was said by some to be different in appearance to the cat who had disappeared.

Andy Warhol once produced a series of cat paintings called '25 cats name (sic) Sam and One Blue Pussy'. Warhol's mother bred Siamese cats while living with her famous son in New York.

Charles Lindbergh, the American aviator, had a black cat called Patsy who was photographed with him in the cockpit of his plane Spirit of St Louis just before his first ever non-stop solo flight from America to Europe. Lindbergh wouldn't take Patsy with him on the flight. 'It is,' he said, 'too dangerous a journey to risk the cat's life.' Nevertheless, Patsy achieved immortality for she was the first domestic cat to appear on a postage stamp. On 10th October 1930, the US Postal Service produced a stamp which included a picture of the Spirit of St Louis, Charles Lindbergh and Patsy.

St Jerome (342-420) was the only Saint known to have kept a cat.
    The following poem was written for children:
If I lost my little cat, I should be sad without it
I should ask St Jerome what to do about it
I should ask St Jerome, just because of that
He's the only saint I know that kept a pussy cat.

Jeremy Bentham, the English philosopher, social reformer, animal lover and renowned eccentric, had a frisky cat called Sir John Langbourne, which was renowned for having a taste for macaroni. As the cat got older he became rather more sedate and a keen churchgoer so Bentham retitled him Rev John Langbourne. Later Bentham gave his cat a doctorate, making him Rev Dr John Langbourne. When the cat finally died Bentham said that he had been very close to becoming a bishop.

Bentham shared his productive life with many cats, each of which was given a human-sounding name with a suitable honorific. Arriving for dinner, Bentham's guests would be ushered into a room where a number of cats were sitting at a table. Guests would be introduced to each cat in turn.

J. M. W. Turner, the English painter who single-handedly created impressionism, had five or six dirty white, pink-eyed tailless cats living with him. When his studio was cleared after his death, many of Turner's drawings were found to have paw prints on them. Turner even used one of his old canvases as a cat flap.

Louis Wain, the famous British cat artist, was an art teacher whose life was changed when, at the age of 21, he was given a black and white kitten called 'Peter'. Peter proved to be far more valuable to Louis Wain than the key to the door would have been. Just before being given the cat Wain had married his younger sister's governess and shortly after their marriage Mrs Wain fell ill. The cat was a great comfort to her. Sitting by her bedside Louis Wain drew Peter and encouraged by his wife, he sent the drawing to the Illustrated London News which published it. Wain's sketches and paintings are now extraordinarily expensive collectors' items. Peter's name was later changed to 'Peter the Great'.

German poet, dramatist, scientist and court official Johann Wolfgang von Goethe wrote a poem about a cat which belonged to Abuherrira, who was one of Mohammed's disciples.

> *Abuherrira's cat, too, is here*
> *Purrs round his master blest,*
> *For holy must the beast appear*
> *The Prophet hath caressed.*

Ernest Hemingway had so many cats (30) that he had a special building erected for them. After a considerable amount of thought the great author (winner of the Nobel Prize for Literature in 1954 for books such as *The Old Man and the Sea, For Whom The Bell Tolls, A Farewell To Arms, The Sun Also Rises* and *A Moveable Feast*) named the special building The Cat House.

When Honey finally caught her tail she wasn't at all sure what to do with it.

Chapter Eighteen

Popular Idioms Referring To Cats

Most of these idioms are English in origin. I have included the meaning of each idiom in parentheses.

1. You look like the cat that swallowed the cream. (You look very pleased with yourself.)

2. To play cat and mouse. (To alternate harshness and leniency.)

3. To be catty. (To be spiteful.)

4. A cat-call. (A whistle of disapproval.)

5. To let the cat out of the bag. (To reveal a secret – sometimes accidentally. The phrase developed when farmers used to sell piglets in sacks. Dealers would pull out one of the piglets and show it to the prospective buyer who, satisfied and assuming that the sack was full of piglets, would hand over his money and totter off home dreaming of endless bacon and egg breakfasts. However, unscrupulous, crooked dealers would sometimes put one or two kittens into the sack along with the piglets. If things went wrong, and the sack was opened accidentally, the cat would escape – giving the game away.)

6. Like a cat on hot bricks. (To be uncomfortable, jumpy, awkward and ill at ease – just as a cat walking on hot bricks would feel and

behave. In America, presumably because they have more bits of tin than bricks, the phrase became 'like a cat on a hot tin roof'.)

7. To wait and see which way the cat jumps. (To remain uncommitted until you see what others think.)

8. A cat-o-nine tails. (A whip with nine leather thongs each of which looked a bit like a cat's tail, was made from cat skin or left marks like the scratches of a cat's paws. Take your pick. In Britain, the cat-o-nine tails was used in the Navy and in the Army and for civilians up until 1948. The whip had nine 'tails' because nine is a special number – a trinity of trinities.)

9. No room to swing a cat. (A small space. The saying came from the fact that sailors who had been sentenced to flogging were punished on deck because there was no room to swing a cat-o-nine tails below deck.)

10. Not a cat in hell's chance. (No chance at all.)

11. Curiosity killed the cat. (Too much curiosity can lead to trouble and might be dangerous.)

12. There's more than one way to skin a cat. This saying is also known as 'There is more than one way to kill a cat'. (There is more than one way to do something. This expression is a shortened version of the saying: 'There are more ways of killing a cat than choking it with cream.' The saying is often used in a rather critical way when someone suggests a long winded or difficult way of doing something.)

13. To lead a cat and dog life. (To quarrel a lot. Commonly used about a husband and wife.)

14. Has the cat got your tongue? (Used about someone who appears to have lost the power of speech – possibly through shyness.)

15. To bell the cat. (To attack a common enemy, although there is risk to yourself, because others will benefit. To offer to put your own life or health at risk in order to help others. The saying is taken from a story which appeared in William Langland's book *The Vision*

Concerning Piers Plowman – a 14th century poem which included the tale of how a group of mice decided to put a bell around the neck of a rather ferocious cat so that they would be warned of its impending arrival. All the mice agreed that this was a splendid idea. But the idea lost some of its attractiveness when one of the mice asked: 'But who is to bell the cat?'.)

16. To put the cat among the pigeons. (To provoke trouble.)

17. A cat burglar. (An agile burglar who climbs up walls, drainpipes etc. and gets into houses through an upper window.)

18. To be made a cat's paw of. (To serve as a tool for someone else. This saying comes from Aesop's fable of the monkey who pulled chestnuts out of the fire with a paw belonging to his friend the cat.)

19. A cat may look at a king. (We are equal. I have as much right to look at you as you at me.)

20. To grin like a Cheshire cat. (To grin widely and often. The saying was first used in Lewis Carroll's classic story Alice in Wonderland. There doesn't seem to be any other origin for the saying though it has been argued that Cheshire cheeses used to be shaped like cats and to have grins on their faces. If you'll believe that you'll believe just about anything. It has also been claimed that cats from Cheshire used to smile a lot because they had special tax privileges. Carroll probably just made that up too.)

21. He thinks he is the cat's whiskers. (He's rather full of himself – and thinks he's the cat's pyjamas. When radio had just been invented the fine wire which made contact with the crystal was known as a cat's whisker (because it looked a bit like one) though just what this has to do with anything I can't imagine.)

22. He thinks he is the cat's pyjamas. (He's rather full of himself – and thinks he's the cat's whiskers. The phrase 'cat's pyjamas' came from America and if he didn't think it up it was almost certainly helped on its way by the world's greatest ever novelist and humorist P.G. Wodehouse who was English to the core.)

23. A wild-cat-strike. (Unofficial strike, organised without the approval of the trade union.)

24. To be a copy-cat. (To imitate someone else.)

25. It's raining cats and dogs. (It's raining a lot. There are several slightly potty theories which attempt to explain this strange saying. One is that the saying originated in the days when the drainage in the streets was so poor that a heavy downpour was likely to flood the streets and to drown dogs and cats. That is one of the most sensible. Whatever the origin, the saying has been traced back to 1653 when a writer called Richard Brome wrote a play called *The City Witt* in which he talked about it raining 'dogs and polecats'.)

26. When the cat's away the mice will play. (An old proverb with origins in numerous countries. It means that when the person in authority is absent those remaining will take advantage of the situation to cause chaos.)

Sarah was planning a night on the tiles so she had had her tail permed.

Chapter Nineteen

How Much Do You Know About Cats?

Choose one answer

1. Cats do not have:
a) a collarbone
b) feet
c) a tail
d) gas bills

2. The collective noun for a litter of kittens is:
a) a lot
b) a nuisance
c) a kindle
d) a delight

3. When running flat out a domestic cat can reach:
a) 31 miles per hour
b) anything it is chasing
c) Glasgow
d) a temperature of 105 degrees Fahrenheit

4. Cats have a total of:
a) 96 toes

b) 26 toes
c) 48 toes
d) 18 toes

5. *The cat flap was invented by:*
a) Winston Churchill
b) Sir Isaac Newton
c) Elvis Presley
d) Christian Dior

6. *How many domestic cats are there estimated to be in the world:*
a) 500 million
b) 152
c) 6
d) quite a lot

7. *How many muscles does a cat have in each ear:*
a) 32
b) 3
c) 786
d) 4,219

8. *People who love cats are known as:*
a) crazy people
b) Jeffrey
c) ailurophiles
d) cat people

9. *If there were such a thing as an average cat, how many hairs per square inch would the average cat possess:*
a) 2
b) 130,000
c) 3
d) 1,999,999

10. Lord Byron travelled around Europe with:
a) five cats
b) a troupe of trapeze artistes
c) a cosmetic surgeon
d) a tank full of goldfish

11. The most popular name for a cat is:
a) Sooty
b) Takeitout!
c) Gerald
d) Kitty

12. Napoleon Bonaparte was terrified of:
a) his mother
b) trains
c) flying
d) cats

13. How many lives are cats reputed to have:
a) two
b) nine
c) as many as they want
d) 2.71

14. A group of grown cats is known as:
a) a flock
b) a chunter
c) a clowder
d) a snooze

15. Neutering a cat
a) extends its lifespan by two or three years
b) brings tears to its eyes
c) really annoys it
d) makes it change colour

16. Cats were introduced to North America by:
a) Woolworths
b) the pilgrims
c) Dick Whittington
d) pirates

17. Cats sometimes walk around with their mouths open because:
a) they like pretending to look stupid
b) they have weak jaw muscles
c) they smell with their mouths as well as their noses
d) they are easily surprised

18. Cats have whiskers ...
a) to make them look debonair
b) to help them see in the dark
c) so that they don't get mistaken for goldfish
d) because they don't shave

19. It was a cat which inspired:
a) Frederic Chopin's to write his *Cat Waltz* (opus 34 number 3)
b) Sir Christopher Wren to build St Paul's Cathedral
c) the designer of the first catamaran
d) the inventor of the mouse trap

20. Which of these animals is not mentioned in the bible:
a) the dog
b) the pig
c) the donkey
d) the cat

21. When their favourite cat died Egyptians used to:
a) go to the top of the highest mountain and wail for a whole night
b) shave off their eyebrows
c) wear sackcloth and ashes for a year
d) have a big party and sacrifice a servant

22. Alexander the Great was terrified of
a) cats
b) sewing needles
c) giraffes
d) buses

23. Cats like to go hunting
a) when the shops are closed
b) just before dawn and just after dusk
c) on Sunday mornings
d) when there is nothing good on the television (as long as the weather is decent)

24. Cats like their food to be served:
a) at room temperature
b) on bone china
c) with a saucer of wine on the side
d) by a man wearing a white waistcoat and carrying a teatowel over his arm

Now check your answers

1. Score 5 if you answered a) or d). Cats do not have collar bones or gas bills. Score 0 if you answered b) or c).

2. Score 5 if you answered c). The collective noun for a little of kittens is 'kindle'. Score 0 if you answered a) or b). You can have 2 points if you answered d) even though it's wrong.

3. Score 5 points if you answered a). When running flat out a domestic cat can reach 31 mph. Score 0 if you chose any other answer.

4. Score 5 if you answered d). Cats have 18 toes (five toes on each front paw, but only four toes on each of the two back paws). Score 0 if you answered a), b) or c).

5. Score 5 if you chose b) Sir Isaac Newton. It was indeed the great

English scientist who invented the cat flap. Score 0 if you chose any of the other possibilities.

6. Score 5 if you answered a) or d). There are thought to be around 500 million domestic cats in the world. (Well, there were when I wrote this book. There will doubtless be more by now. Score 0 if you answered b) or c).

7. Score 5 if you answered a). A cat has 32 muscles in each ear. Score 0 if you chose any of the other possibilities.

8. Score 5 if you chose c). Cat lovers are known as ailurophiles. You can have 2 points if you answered d) but keep quiet about it. Score 0 if you chose either of the others.

9. Score 5 if you answered b). The average cat (if such a creature existed) would have around 130,000 hairs per square inch. Score 0 if you chose any other answer.

10. Score 5 if you answered a). Lord Byron travelled around Europe with five cats and was a braver man than I am. Score 0 if you answered anything else.

11. Score 5 if you answered a). The most popular name for a cat is Sooty. Score 0 if you chose any other answer.

12. Score 5 if you answered d). Napoleon Bonaparte never backed away from a battle but he was terrified of cats. Score 0 if you answered anything else

13. Score 5 if you chose b). Cats are reputed to have nine lives and if you didn't get this one right you can't have been paying attention. Score absolutely 0 if you chose any other answer and think yourself lucky you haven't had points deducted and aren't being kept in after school to clean out all the cat trays.

14. Score 5 if you answered c). A group of grown cats is known as a clowder. Score 0 if you answered anything else.

15. Score 5 if you answered a). Neutering a cat is said to extend its lifespan by two to three years. Score 0 for any other answer.

16. Score 5 if you answered b). Cats were introduced into North America by the pilgrims. Score 0 for any other answer.

17. Score 5 if you answered c). Cats often walk around with their mouths open because they smell through their mouths as well as their noses. Score 0 for any other answer.

18. Score 5 if you answered b). Although cats do use their whiskers to help decide whether or not they can get through a gap they also use their whiskers to help them move around when the light is poor. Cats' whiskers are so sensitive that they can detect the very slightest movement in air currents. As a cat walks in the dark its whiskers will pick up small eddies in the air caused by its own movement. The disturbed air guides the cat and helps it move around without bumping into things. A cat's whiskers help it to 'see' in the dark. Score 0 for any other answer.

19. Score 5 if you answered a). It was a cat which inspired Frederic Chopin's to write his *Cat Waltz* (opus 34 number 3). Score 0 for any other answer.

20. Score 5 if you answered d). The cat is the only one of these animals not mentioned in the bible. Score 0 for any other answer.

21. Score 5 if you answered b). If a much loved cat died an Egyptian would shave off his eyebrows. Score 0 for other answers.

22. Score 5 if you answered a). Alexander the Great was terrified of cats. Score 0 for any other answer.

23. Score 5 if you answered b). Cats prefer to go hunting just before

dawn and just after dusk. Their eyesight, which is particularly good in dim light, gives them an advantage at these times. Score 0 if you chose a), c) or d).

24. Score 5 if you answered a). Cats prefer their food to be served at room temperature – not too hot and not too cold. Score 0 if you chose any other answer.

Now check your score:

If you scored 100 to 120:
Congratulations. You know a great deal about cats and are now entitled to put the letters C.E. after your name. (If you haven't worked it out the letters C.E. stand for Cat Expert.)

If you scored 60 to 95:
So near and yet so far. I expect you're kicking yourself. I bet you really knew the right answers and would have scored higher if you'd thought a bit more. I'm a generous person: if you give me your personal assurance that you really knew the answers to some of the questions you got wrong you can upgrade yourself. (Now see above.)

If you scored under 60:
Do you remember that awful phrase 'could do better'? Well, I'm afraid that what's you get for scoring under 60. Still, the consolation is that you now know all the answers. So rub out your first set of replies and do the quiz again. You should do much better second time around and you can show your revised results to all your friends.

Note: This questionnaire has been given two dozen questions so as not to conform with EU regulations requiring everything to be metric. I would sell bananas by the pound if I could but since I'm not in the greengrocery business I have to make my voice heard in my own small way.

Chapter Twenty

Tiddles and Tiddlelina

*Tiddles found herself in the middle of a dark forest. At first she was
rather frightened. And then she smelt a foot she recognised and immediately
felt much better.*

"Some days," thought Tiddles, "life really isn't too bad at all."

Tiddles and Tiddlelina talked to each other on
the phone all the time.

Tiddles was very proud of his Upright, who had won many prizes in Upright Shows.

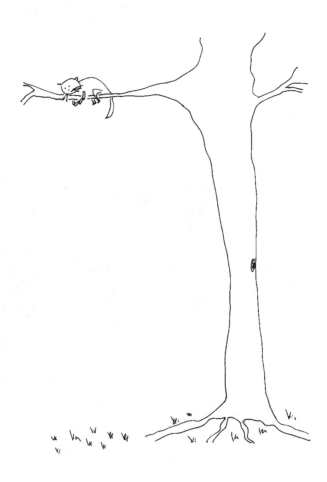

Tiddles could never understand why 'down' always seemed
so much further than 'up'.

Tiddles was always keen to greet his Upright enthusiastically.
He did not believe in hiding his emotions.

Finding himself alone with the Christmas turkey, Tiddles was suddenly overcome by uncertainty. He simply didn't know where to start.

"At last," thought Tiddles.
"Something good on the TV."

"I've put on a little weight," said Tiddles. "So I've had *myself* measured standing on a stool. The results show that for my height I am terribly under-nourished and should eat more fish.

*After the Uprights had gone to bed, Tiddles and Tiddlelina went round
to the back of the TV set to see if they could find any of the little
mouse-sized people who lived inside it.*
"Some of them look quite plump and tasty," said Tiddles.

When Tiddles and Tiddlelina went to look at the statue of the Unknown
Cat they were upset to see a bird perched on the statue's head. "How
disrespectful," said Tiddles

*The day before Ascot someone sat on Dottatina's new hat.
"Don't worry," said Tiddles "stick a flower in my ear and
I'll be your hat for the day. Everyone will be very impressed
and you'll probably get your picture in the papers."*

Tiddles wins the Olympic long-jump (with added vase complication).

Tiddles and Tiddlelina were having their first party and had prepared quite a good selection of goodies for their guests.

Tiddles didn't much mind the fetching jumper his Upright made him wear in cold weather. But he hated the matching tail warmer (with added bobble) and refused to go out of the house wearing it.

"Now I can say I've been on TV,"
thought Tiddles

*Thanks to Tiddles, Harold managed to hide his
rapidly developing baldness from all but his most
intimate acquaintances.*

Tiddles often felt completely alone, even when he was not, in truth, alone at all.

"There are far too many fat cats around," said Tiddles. "So, to stop them getting
any fatter, I've collected all the fish and brought them here."
"Goody," said Tiddlelina. "Shall we have them for tea?"

Chapter Twenty One

Twenty One Ways To Make Your Cat Love You For Ever

1. Cats can be just as fussy about the water they drink as they are about the food they eat (or the laps they sit on). To make your cat love you, make sure that you give him or her the type of water he or she loves. The water should be served at room temperature since cat's don't like water which is too warm or too cold. It definitely shouldn't reek of chlorine or anything else. Cats are very sensitive to the smell of chlorine (and other chemicals) in tap water – that's why they often go outside and drink rainwater from a seemingly dirty puddle rather than drink apparently clean water from their bowl. If you really want your cat to adore you splash out on bottled, natural spring water. Cats don't drink a great deal and this won't cost you a fortune.

2. Give your cat loads of cuddles and strokes. Cats love physical signs of affection. And if you want to create a bond with a cat this is one of the best ways to do it.

    I 'bonded' with Alice (the author of *Alice's Diary* and *The Adventures of Alice*) after she had fallen into a lavatory bowl as a kitten. Identifying its purpose she had tried to use it herself, in preference to the neatly raked tray of expensive cat litter which had been provided for her, and had overbalanced and fallen into the water. The slippery porcelain sides meant that she couldn't climb out. When I pulled her out of the toilet bowl she was sopping wet. I slipped her inside my shirt to dry out and warm up and by the time she was ready to emerge from my shirt the bonding process was complete. She recognised and appreciated my gesture and became a friend for life.

Not many cats will need rescuing in this way, but stroking and cuddling a cat will make it happy. And a happy cat will usually love you for ever. It is, generally, true to say that the more an Upright cares for a cat the more attention the cat will pay to the Upright.

(Note: Alice loved a warm cuddle so much that she learned how to switch on my electric typewriter when I was out of the room or the house. She liked the typewriter because it made a purring sound and got quite warm after being switched on for a few minutes. I discovered that she had learned how to do this when I repeatedly entered my study and found my typewriter switched on. At first I thought I'd simply forgotten to switch it off but one day I popped back unexpectedly and saw her operating the switch which turned the machine on. It was a small switch that I found rather stiff and difficult to operate but Alice didn't seem to have much trouble with it. She loved that typewriter and was noticeably upset when it broke down and had to be replaced with my first computer.)

3. Don't put out too much food when feeding a cat. Some Uprights try to make their own lives simpler by putting out a whole day's ration of food in the morning. Yuk. Would you like your whole day's food supplies to be put out on a plate at breakfast time?

   Whether it is canned or fresh food, the entire day's ration should not be put out at one time, because what is left over will become stale, dry and probably contaminated.

   Leftovers should be taken away when a cat has finished and the food bowl cleaned ready for the next meal.

   Opened cans of food should be kept in the refrigerator but taken out about half an hour before feeding time to give the food in them a chance to reach room temperature. Remember that cats do not like their food chilled. They prefer it at 'mouse' temperature.

4. Never, ever, laugh at a cat. Cats are extremely sensitive and easily embarrassed. For example, a cat who misjudges a jump and ends up in an undignified heap on the floor will invariably be very put

out, and will often retire to comfort itself with a self-grooming session. Similarly a cat who has had to retreat after a confrontation with a strange feline will often become preoccupied with cleaning his or her tail. Never laugh in such circumstances. When they are afraid or embarrassed cats become (literally) hot and bothered. They lick themselves to help cool down. If you laugh at a cat he or she may never forget.

5. Remember that your cat depends upon you for food, health, welfare and happiness. If you are fortunate enough to look after a cat you have a great responsibility to give the cat a reasonable share of your attention and time. You should not allow a cat into your life if you do not have attention and time which you are prepared to give.

6. If you keep your cat indoors (as increasingly numbers of Uprights do) make sure that you provide a scratching post, unless you are happy to see your furniture ruined. Cats need to scratch to keep their claws under control and a bored cat, or one who is kept indoors without a scratching post, can do a remarkable amount of damage to furniture.

7. Don't expect a cat to eat chocolate or puddings. Most cats don't have much of a sweet tooth and seem to have a low tolerance for sugar in their diet. Too much sugar is likely to result in diarrhoea – a problem which can be unpleasant for both cat and Upright.

8. It is something of a myth that cats love milk. Uprights are the only creatures who habitually drink milk produced by another species. Although most cats will drink cows' milk the lactose content can easily upset them. Water is usually a better drink – and certainly one less likely to cause a digestive upset.

9. If you share your life with a cat think carefully before introducing any other animal (cat or not) into the household. Cats do not take kindly to the introduction of other animals into a home where they have established themselves. How would you like it if you came home and found an elephant or a skunk ensconced in your living room? How would you react if you popped in out of the garden and found complete strangers sitting in your living room watching

your television set? Even the introduction of a baby into the household can be very disturbing – however comfortable and well established the cat might feel. When faced with this kind of stress, or indeed any unusual behaviour among the Uprights in the household, there is a risk that a cat may hide or even disappear for good. To minimise this risk you should remember to make a big fuss of the cat whenever you are making changes to your household. Let the cat know that, whatever else is happening around it, he or she is still loved.

10. Cats are conservatives (as far as I know, only with a small 'c'). They are creatures of habit and they like patterns in their lives. They do not like change. They hate surprises. They like things to stay the same, and they like things to happen at the same time every day. If you move the furniture around, bring in new furniture, or introduce a new shed or garden seat within an outdoor cat's home range, you must expect the cat to investigate thoroughly. You should also expect some scent-marking to take place. Try to introduce changes gradually.

11. Cats dislike deep, bowl-shaped containers. They cannot see what is happening around them when they are eating and this makes them feel nervous. To make sure that a cat feels comfortable when feeding, choose wide, fairly shallow-sided dishes. And choose dishes which are heavy enough not to be knocked over or to slide around when being licked. A cat who is enjoying his or her food doesn't want to have to chase his or her food bowl for yards across the linoleum.

12. Be consistent. And make sure that all the Uprights in a household are consistent. Cats can live with rules (for example, knowing that they aren't allowed into bedrooms) as long as the rules are kept. If one member of the family permits something which another prohibits a cat can become confused and stressed. If one Upright allows a cat to lie on a bed and another doesn't the cat will (quite reasonably) get very confused. Consistency is as important with cats as it is with children.

13. If the cat who lives with you isn't allowed out of doors he or she will still want to go hunting – even if it is the feline equivalent of

drag hunting. Hunting is a vital part of any cat's life and cats who live inside will appreciate the chance to chase a ball or a piece of paper tied to wool. Allow some time each day for a little hunting practice. Cats who are denied this sort of action are likely to become bored or even depressed.

14. Cats, like the rest of us, need their own private space. Each cat needs to feel that it is totally in control within its personal and private space and that it can choose what goes on there and who or what should be admitted. Just as children like to feel that their bedroom space is sacrosanct so a cat will need to have a hideaway which is not likely to be invaded by bags of shopping, bundles of dirty washing, muddy football boots or a bag of golf clubs. It is to this private space that a cat will go if it is stressed. Cats will usually find their own favourite private space – usually in a quiet part of the house where he or she can rest or sleep, or quietly observe life passing by, without being disturbed. Try to respect the cat's choice if you can.

15. If you are out of the home all day and your cat is allowed to live outside as well as inside, do make sure that you have a cat flap fitted. Cats do not understand the concept of doors. They like to feel that they go in when they want and out when they want. (On the other hand, cats which never go out of the home will soon grow accustomed to the idea that their world ends at the front door. They will, however, still want to have freedom to roam within their domain.)

16. If you give a cat a collar then make sure that the collar is elasticated, or has an elastic section which will enable the cat to wriggle free if, for example, it gets caught in a tree. Cats have been strangled by their collars. It is obviously much better for a cat to lose its collar than for you to lose your cat.

17. Even if it is intended that a cat should live an indoor life there is absolutely no way of guaranteeing, even in the most careful household, that the cat will not escape. It is important, therefore, that even indoor cats should wear some form of identification.

Just make sure that if you use a collar to carry whatever form of identification you choose you select an elasticated collar from which the cat can, if necessary, wriggle free.

18. Cats respond better to higher pitched voices and consequently, therefore, tend to prefer women's voices or children's voices to deep male voices. Men can make themselves more popular with cats by speaking in a higher voice than usual.

19. Never, ever, under any circumstances, give your cat cheap food. I have seen secret advice given to young cats by a panel of experienced, older cats. The advice states, quite clearly, that when unsatisfactory food is provided a cat should, whenever possible, turn up its nose and walk away. If, however, hunger drives the cat to eat cheap food it should regurgitate as much of it as possible within thirty minutes. The advice given states that the regurgitating cat should give no more than 30 seconds notice ('enough time to cause alarm and even panic but not enough time to enable the Upright to make appropriate plans or actually do anything other than watch') and should, whenever possible, vomit on carpet rather than linoleum or kitchen tiles. 'Tufted or shagpile carpet is preferable for this purpose,' concludes the advice. You have been warned.

20. Make a big fuss of your cat if you have to take him or her somewhere that he or she doesn't want to go (e.g. the vet).

   Cats can develop a real aversion to people they don't like. And they often take a dislike to people who make them do things they don't want to do.

   After a professor in New York noticed that his cat hated him for days every time he took her to the vet he persuaded a female friend to take the cat to the vet on his behalf. As planned, the cat started to hate the friend instead of the professor. But the hatred grew and grew. Eventually, the professor could tell when his friend was coming – even though she was some distance away from his home – because his cat would run and hide. The cat did this even though the woman was not in sight, not within hearing and smelling range and not planning to take the cat to the vet.

21. Accepting that a cat is independent and proud is fundamental to the development of a healthy relationship between a cat and an Upright. Cats also like to feel that their Uprights don't take them for granted. A cat expects an Upright to take – and enjoy – a subservient role in the relationship and if the Upright attempts to avoid his or her responsibilities this will not be well received.

For example, a cat who has always had doors opened for him by his Upright may not welcome the introduction of a cat flap. The cat flap may well make everyone's life easier (the cat can go in and out whenever he or she wants to and the Upright doesn't have to keep opening and shutting the door) but to the cat the important thing is that there has been a significant and unacceptable change in the relationship between cat and Upright.

So, under these circumstances, the cat may simply insist on waiting by the door – ignoring the existence of the cat flap. Repeatedly showing the cat how the flap works will not make any difference. The cat knows exactly what the cat flap is for, and how to use it, but will still insist on having the door opened for him when he or she wants to come in or go out. This will be a matter of principle, not practicality.

The only hope for the Upright is that the cat will eventually decide that it is in its own interests to use the flap. Trying to hurry up this process by refusing to open the door, or by constantly pushing the cat flap to and fro, will simply delay the happy ending. No Upright should ever imagine, not for one second, that he or she can be as stubborn as a cat.

Best of friends

Chapter Twenty Two

Rhymes And Love Letters

Friendship

Most cats that I've known
(And I've known quite a few)
Have enjoyed many pleasures
(Eating and sleeping, to name but two)
But the thing in this life
(And the next, probably too)
Which has given most joy
(To them and to me and probably you)
Is the simplest and plainest
(It's odd but its true)
Nothing exceeds the delight that is given
(Neither pleasure that's old nor pleasure that's new)
By the warmth and the passion of genuine friendship
(That started slow but gradually grew).

Missing But Still Here

I miss you my sweet kitten
Even more than I did fear
I miss your playful ways
Now that you're no longer here

You were always ever joyful
Never quiet and never still
Full of fun and mischief
And hunting for a thrill

I miss you my sweet kitten
But I love you as before
Now you're fully grown
You're my friend for evermore

My Upright Is A Queen

My Upright is a Queen
Sweet, generous, true and good
She never could be mean
To harm she never would

She never misses tea
No doors are ever shut
Her affection's all for me
There never is a 'but'

Her lap is always warm
The fire is ever lit
Kindness is the norm
'Cus I'm her favourite kit

My life is never bad
And I give thanks to him above
I'm very, very glad
That I have her golden love

The Happy Cat

The happiest cat in the world
Lay neatly in front of the fire
Her whiskers were trim, her tail was curled
And her happiness was entire

She had a loving Upright
And a quiet and peaceful home
She never knew of hunger
And she had no cause to roam

Then she met a wild-born cat
A wanderer, never tamed
He said she was a prisoner
And she felt herself ashamed

She thought of running off
And leaving all she knew
She thought she'd find her freedom
If she started life anew

(continued)

(continued)

She knew that she could hunt
And feed herself each day
She was sure she would survive
In her new life as a stray

But when she looked around
And explored her present bliss
She knew it was her Upright
Who'd be the one thing that she'd miss

The shame she'd felt now left her
And she knew that she would stay
Because her Upright's love
Would give life to every day

The Dancing Kitten

She dances
Like a moonbeam
So light
She seems to have no weight
A wisp
Floating on the breeze
But when
After many tries
She succeeds
In jumping onto the mantelpiece
The crash
Of a vase breaking in the hearth
Shatters the silence
She is then neither moonbeam nor wisp
That dancing kitten

Cats, Cats, Cats

Orange, black and white
Large, medium and small
They wander out at night
And ignore you when you call

Shut them in in error
And the room will soon be wrecked
They'll wage a war of terror
And you know what to expect

Regardless of their colour
Regardless of their size
Cats are their own masters
And inordinately wise.

What I love

I love
Each tiny velvet paw, each whisker and each purr
Each and every touch of your soft, exquisite fur
I love
The exquisite roughness of your tongue as it rasps upon my skin
The way you reach and touch me with one slowly outstretched paw
The way you curl your tail and wrap it round your nose
I love
Each minute we spend together, each hour and every day
Each memory we share, every moment, every way
I love

The Days

She awoke
before the sun had properly risen into the sky,
to fully illuminate the day.
She rushed out into the garden
while the grass was still wet
and cobwebs glistened with morning dew.
She spent the day chasing feathers,
climbing trees, racing after leaves.
She did not go back into the house
until the sun had set,
turning out the light
and leaving the world as dark
as it had been
before the day had started.
She had enjoyed the day
because she enjoyed her life.
She always enjoyed her days,
for she knew they *were* her life.

Cat heaven

Also by Vernon Coleman
Alice's Diary

Well over 40,000 delighted readers from around the world have bought this wonderful book which tells of a year in the life of a mixed tabby cat called Alice.

Alice records the year's events and disasters with great humour and insight and at long last gives us a glimpse of what it is really like to be a cat.

Our files are bursting with letters from confirmed 'Alice' fans (adults and children alike) who tell us how much they have enjoyed this book.

Delightfully illustrated throughout (with just a little help from one of the Uprights) and is an absolute must for animal and cat lovers everywhere.

"*Alice's Diary* is one of the nicest books I have ever read. She has wonderful insight."
(Mrs J., London)

"Please send copies of *Alice's Diary* to the eleven friends on the accompanying list. It is a wonderful book which will give them all great pleasure."
(Mr R., Lancashire)

"One of the most delightful cat books in the world!"
(Mrs M. R., Australia)

Price £9.99 (hardback)

Published by Chilton Designs
Order from Publishing House • Trinity Place • Barnstaple • Devon
EX32 9HG • England
Telephone 01271 328892 • Fax 01271 328768

Also by Vernon Coleman

Alice's Adventures

After the publication of her first book, Alice was inundated with fan mail and requests urging her to put paw to paper once more. The result is this, her second volume of memoirs.

In her second book she records yet more adventures and mishaps with many a tear being shed during this eventful year.

Full of the illustrations and humour so much-loved by readers of her first book.

"I didn't think Alice could surpass her first book – but she has. I really loved *Alice's Adventures*. The saddest moment came when I finished it. When will the next volume be ready?"
(Mrs K., Somerset)

"We have had cats for over 30 years and Alice describes incidents which are so real that we nearly died laughing at them."
(Mrs O., Leeds)

"*Alice's Adventures* is the loveliest book I have ever read. It captures everything brilliantly. Thinking back over the book I can't help smiling. I have never enjoyed a book as much."
(Mrs H., Edinburgh)

Price £9.99 (hardback)

Published by Chilton Designs
Order from Publishing House • Trinity Place • Barnstaple • Devon
EX32 9HG • England
Telephone 01271 328892 • Fax 01271 328768

Also by Vernon Coleman

Alice and Other Friends

Thousands of readers have already discovered the joys of *Alice's Diary* and *Alice's Adventures* which have sold tens of thousands of copies and entranced animal lovers all over the world.

Vernon Coleman 'helped' Alice to write and illustrate these two books. Now, at last, here is Vernon Coleman's own account of life with Alice and her half sister Thomasina.

Charming, touching and intensely personal, this book is packed with stories, anecdotes and reminiscences about Alice and the many other creatures Vernon Coleman has met, known and lived with. There are, of course, many stories about Vernon Coleman's four pet sheep. The book is liberally and beautifully illustrated with numerous line drawings by the author.

Price £12.99 (hardback)

Sheep do not like the rain

Published by Chilton Designs
Order from Publishing House • Trinity Place • Barnstaple • Devon
EX32 9HG • England
Telephone 01271 328892 • Fax 01271 328768

Also by Vernon Coleman

We Love Cats

If you love cats then you'll absolutely adore Vernon Coleman's latest book, *We Love Cats* – it's a real celebration of cats!

Following on in the tradition of Vernon Coleman's other cat books (*Alice's Diary* and *Alice's Adventures*) *We Love Cats* is packed with humour and insight into the way cats think, behave and quietly run our lives.

We Love Cats contains over 100 new and original squiggly Vernon Coleman drawings (he calls them 'catoons') plus loads of poems, limericks and amazing facts about cats. It will make a superb gift for any cat or animal lover. But, be warned: if you buy one you won't want to give it away!

In *We Love Cats* you will discover over 100 fascinating facts about cats, and the truth about some popular cat myths. Below, are just some of the facts that you can read about:

♦   Famous people who loved cats.
♦   What does it mean when a cat sleeps in a certain position?
♦   Why talking to your cat isn't as daft as people think.
♦   Find out how cats really prefer to have their food served.
♦   Famous people who were frightened of cats.
♦   Something about the cat-flap which may surprise you.
♦   Why your cat may refuse to drink your tap water.
♦   Do cats really need milk?
♦   Find out what's so special about your cat's nose pad.
♦   What do cats, camels and giraffes all have in common?

And much, much, more!
Price £12.99 (hardback)

Published by Chilton Designs
Order from Publishing House • Trinity Place • Barnstaple • Devon
EX32 9HG • England
Telephone 01271 328892 • Fax 01271 328768

Also by Vernon Coleman

The Secret Lives of Cats

The Secret Lives of Cats consists of selected letters between two cats: Lemon-Coloured Lion Heart with Long Fine Whiskers and his mother.

Cats don't write letters, of course. They don't take a pen and a piece of paper, jot down their thoughts, fears, news and dreams, fold the paper, put it into an envelope, seal the envelope, add an address and a stamp and then put the resultant slim packet into a post box. Cats can, and do, communicate with one another (and can do so over long distances) but they don't need to do so by sending one another letters.

Cats communicate with one another using their own effective, efficient form of telepathy called 'felipathy'.

Many cat lovers have often expressed innocent astonishment at the amount of time cats spend sleeping. The cats are, in fact, frequently busy exchanging messages with other cats. The twitches and involuntary movements which can often be observed among sleeping cats are simply signs that they are, in fact, engaged in an unusually hectic and, perhaps, emotionally-charged conversation with another cat.

This is the first time Uprights have ever been allowed access to the private correspondence exchanged by cats. *The Secret Lives of Cats* is full of wisdom and humour. You'll laugh at Lemon's innocence and his mother's wise answers and you'll hold your breath as Lemon faces the biggest challenge of his life. This book will make you smile, cry and, at the end, feel warm all over.

Illustrated by the author
Price £12.99 (hardback)

Published by Chilton Designs
Order from Publishing House • Trinity Place • Barnstaple • Devon
EX32 9HG • England
Telephone 01271 328892 • Fax 01271 328768

Also by Vernon Coleman

The Cats' Own Annual

Vernon claims (and we don't like to disagree with him about this) that there is a newspaper for cats called *Cats' Own Paper,* which is only available for cat subscribers. Vernon insists that to celebrate the newspaper's centenary he was been asked to compile an Annual so that 'Uprights' can see the world through a cat's eyes.

Here are just a few of the things you'll find inside this wonderful book...

♦ Reasons why cats are better than dogs
♦ Facts every cat-lover will want to know
♦ Best things about Uprights
♦ Worst things about Uprights
♦ Foods cats really like
♦ Foods cats really hate
♦ Quotes about cats
♦ Ways in which cats are superior to Uprights
♦ An ordinary day in the life of a cat
♦ The Cat Rules
♦ How you can extend your cat's lifespan by two or three years
♦ Problem pages for cats (and for Uprights)
♦ Poems and limericks

Finally, *The Cats' Own Annual* also includes a beautiful and very special prayer for cats.

Price £12.99 (hardback)

Published by Chilton Designs
Order from Publishing House • Trinity Place • Barnstaple • Devon
EX32 9HG • England
Telephone 01271 328892 • Fax 01271 328768

Also by Vernon Coleman

The Bilbury Chronicles

A young doctor arrives to begin work in the small village of Bilbury. This picturesque hamlet is home to some memorable characters who have many a tale to tell, and Vernon Coleman weaves together a superb story full of humour and anecdotes. The Bilbury books will transport you back to the days of old-fashioned, traditional village life where you never needed to lock your door, and when a helping hand was only ever a moment away. The first novel in the series.

"I am just putting pen to paper to say how very much I enjoyed The Bilbury Chronicles. I just can't wait to read the others."
(Mrs K., Cambs)

"...a real delight from cover to cover. As the first in a series it holds out the promise of entertaining things to come."
(Daily Examiner)

"The Bilbury novels are just what I've been looking for. They are a pleasure to read over and over again."
(Mrs C., Lancs)

Price £12.99 (hardback)

Published by Chilton Designs
Order from Publishing House • Trinity Place • Barnstaple • Devon
EX32 9HG • England
Telephone 01271 328892 • Fax 01271 328768

Also by Vernon Coleman

Second Innings

The characters leap from the page as they draw you in to this tale of a young man (Biffo Brimstone) who overcomes the adversity of modern day living by, quite simply, running away! He leaves an unrewarding job, a shrewish and demanding wife and a couple of surly children and takes the next train out of the miserable suburban estate which has been his home for the past few years of his mundane life.

The train takes him to a part of the country he has never before visited, and the subsequent bus journey deposits him in the village of Fondling-under-Water. It is there that his new life begins.

"A piece of good old-fashioned escapism, an easy-to-follow plot; just right to relax with after a busy day ... you would be happy to lend it to your granny or anyone else's granny come to that. This author has the ability to create a distinctive 'mind's eye' picture of every character. The story would 'translate' into an excellent radio play."
(The Journal of the Cricket Society)

"Settling down with Vernon Coleman's latest novel is one of the best restorative treatments I know for relieving the stresses and strains of modern living. Right from page one you can feel yourself unwind as you enjoy the antics of the wonderful array of characters and their exploits. Terrific reading for anyone." *(Lincolnshire Echo)*

Price £14.99 (hardback)

Published by Chilton Designs
Order from Publishing House • Trinity Place • Barnstaple • Devon
EX32 9HG • England
Telephone 01271 328892 • Fax 01271 328768

For a catalogue of Vernon Coleman's books
please write to:

Publishing House
Trinity Place
Barnstaple
Devon EX32 9HG
England

Telephone   01271 328892
Fax   01271 328768

Outside the UK:
Telephone   +44 1271 328892
Fax   +44 1271 328768

Or visit our website:

www.vernoncoleman.com